THE
NEW LIFE WORK MODEL

PRACTICE
GUIDE

WRITTEN AND CREATED

BY

EDITH A. NICHOLLS

Russell House Publishing

First published in 2005 by:

Russell House Publishing Ltd.

4 St. George's House

Uplyme Road

Lyme Regis

Dorset DT7 3LS

Tel: 01297-443948

Fax: 01297-442722

e-mail: help@russellhouse.co.uk

www.russellhouse.co.uk

© Edith Nicholls

The moral right of Edith Nicholls to be identified as the author of this work has been asserted by her in accordance with The Copyright, Designs and Patents Act 1988.

British Library Cataloguing-in-publication Data:

A catalogue record for this book is available from the British Library.

ISBN: 1-903855-81-0, 978-1-903855-81-2

Printed in Great Britain by CPI Group (UK) Ltd, Croydon, CR0 4YY

All names, dates of birth, addresses and places used in this guide are entirely fictitious and any resemblance to persons and situations is purely coincidental.

About Russell House Publishing

RHP is a group of social work, probation, education and youth and community work practitioners and academics working in collaboration with a professional publishing team.

Our aim is to work closely with the field to produce innovative and valuable materials to help managers, trainers, practitioners and students.

We are keen to receive feedback on publications and new ideas for future projects.

For details of our other publications please visit our website or ask us for a catalogue. Contact details are on this page.

CONTENTS

ABOUT THIS GUIDE

'Life can only be understood backwards
but must be lived forwards.'

Sören Kierkegaard,
author and poet (1813 - 1855)

Not a social work quote but one that encapsulates the whole philosophy and ethos of Life Work. For some children who have been separated from their birth families the picture they see when looking backwards is a gaping void. How, then, can they possibly begin to understand their life and move forwards?

This New Life Work Model aims to help those children make sense of their life and more ably face the challenges the future may bring.

This guide is to help agencies bring about a change in practice and a new way to deliver quality Life Work. Every practitioner, carer and adoptive parent should own a copy.

One of the main components of The New Life Work Model is the preservation of children's memories whilst separated from their birth family and being looked after. To achieve the goal of this component 'My Memory Books' are available. There are currently three different types of memory books: one for babies and toddlers, one for children age 4+ and one for children age 8+. They can be purchased from Russell House Publishing

The guide is divided into five chapters each one dealing with a different aspect of the New Life Work Model.

Chapter 1—Introduction to the New Life Work Model

This chapter deals with the purpose of Life Work and its theoretical base. It examines how and why agencies have failed or are failing to meet the Life Work needs of *all* children separated from birth family.

It looks at why there is a need for change in delivering Life Work and what Life Work should be. It explores how the New Life Work Model meets the needs of all children separated from their birth family and explains the role of temporary primary carers.

Chapter 2—The Process and Components of The New Life Work Model

This chapter deals with the process and components of the New Life Work Model, and how the Life Work needs of children are met by the model. It then examines the individual components in more detail.

It begins by examining the care planning process and details how the New Life Work Model integrates with this process, what the Life Work needs of children separated from birth families are and how the model meets these needs. It identifies the main and secondary components of the model then details each of them individually, explaining their purpose and aims and how agencies can set them in operation.

THE NEW LIFE WORK MODEL
PRACTICE GUIDE

Chapter 3—Creating Family History Books

This chapter is entirely devoted to the purpose and creation of Family History Books. It sets out in detail on where to begin, what needs to be done and how to present this information in a form that would interest a child and promote their genetic identity.

THE NEW LIFE WORK MODEL
PRACTICE GUIDE

Chapter 4—The Role of Temporary Primary Carers

This chapter looks at how the New Life Work Model recognises the important role temporary primary carers perform and explains their responsibilities within the model and how they can fulfil those responsibilities. It offers guidance on how to give children information and explanations as to why they are looked after and the reasons for their separation from their birth family. Using the clear theoretical base of Fahlberg's 3 part parenting model (1994) it explains how to create a game that could help a child's understanding of these complex matters.

It also explains how the New Life Work Model acknowledges the carers feelings within the moving on stage of caring for a child and provides a booklet 'Moving On', highlighting survival points for carers.

Chapter 5—Assisting Adopters in the Telling Process

This chapter is about assisting adopters in the 'telling process' which not only includes the telling and meaning of adoption but also the giving of information and explanation.

It provides a booklet 'Talking to your Children' which acknowledges the difficulties adopters face within the telling process and offers guidelines on how to overcome some of the barriers to informing and explaining adult matters to children within the framework of a lifelong process.

ABOUT THE AUTHOR

And The Creation Of The New Life Work Model

> **IDENTITY IS...**
>
> "...a complex and intangible phenomena, taken for granted when we have it and yet desperately sought after when we are denied it. It is a myriad of interconnecting fragments of memory and experience, one's own and those of other people. Many of these memories and experiences preceded one's own existence."
>
> – Nicholls 2005

I am an adoption support social worker with Knowsley MBC on Merseyside. I have over 24 years experience in social work and qualified in 1987 from Liverpool Polytechnic. I have worked in education, generic social work, child protection and eventually specialising in the field of adoption and fostering.

Whilst, throughout my social work career, I have undertaken numerous training and study courses I believe the three year studies I undertook with the Merseyside Psychotherapy Institute, in conjunction with the Tavistock Clinic, on exploring the unconscious, personality development, psychoanalytical theory and child development research, has had the most impact on my social work practice.

My interest in Life Work for children separated from their birth families has its roots in both my professional and personal life.

I have witnessed first hand the damaging effects on children who have had their genetic identity denied or erased or who have not been given the opportunity to grieve for the loss of and separation from their families of birth, even when they have no recollection or memory of them.

The effects are far reaching, not just in childhood but well into adulthood even for the child who is loved and wanted in their new family and may well have identified strongly with them.   I began to feel frustrated by the deficiencies in practice in relation to this issue recognising that this owed more to bureaucratic or institutional failings than to practitioners themselves.

In the changing face of child care legislation and the subsequent recommendations for social work practice it became almost impossible to develop any creative and innovative skills outside the rigidity of the child protection framework. The result of which was the demise of any meaningful Life Work unless practitioners were willing and/or able to undertake this work outside of their contractual agreement with their employer.

That's where it began for me—creating life books in my own time for two young sisters moving on to adoption. This, I thought, was crazy and that I was probably not the only social worker giving up the pleasures of watching Coronation Street for a long night time appointment with the kitchen table writing and painting Life Books. Or spending my Saturdays being chauffeured around by my husband (because it was easier to take photos without having to drive) across the Merseyside area taking photographs of places that were of significance to the children.

I began to question why this situation had developed and as the questioning went on the answers became clearer.

After many years of research we, in the social work sense of 'we', had not learned to begin Life Work when it mattered, that is from the very moment a child is separated from their family and that, despite a very clearly defined care planning process, we still hadn't included the need for Life Work within this process. Life Work has become an after thought, something that had to be done only when a child was at the point of moving on to permanence. How then were we meeting the needs of *all* children separated from their birth families, and what about promoting genetic identity and lifelong needs? These questions led to the embryonic stage of the New Life Work Model.

Whilst the problem appeared complex I found the solution surprisingly simple: make Life Work part of the care planning process, create shared responsibility for its completion and broaden its narrow focus of immediate need to that of lifelong needs.

The New Life Work Model was born...

ACKNOWLEDGEMENTS

* To my dear and wonderful late husband John for faithfully believing in me and for giving me the confidence and motivation to set down in words my beliefs and theories.

* To my daughter Lynn, my grandson Andrew and my late son John for being such remarkable and special people and for giving me undiluted and continued inspiration.

* To my colleague Carol Evans for her knowledge of adoption issues.

* To Ann Wheal for her time and invaluable guidance.

* To Russell House Publishing for their patience and understanding of the importance of Life Work and giving me the opportunity to share this model with carers, professionals and adopters.

* And to all those children, separated from their families of birth, with whom I have had the inspirational experience of having met and/or worked with, for giving me dedication.

PRACTICE GUIDE

CHAPTER 1

INTRODUCTION TO THE NEW LIFE WORK MODEL

THE NEW LIFE WORK MODEL

Its Purpose, Theoretical Base And Application

F rom Brodzinskey et al.(1993).

'Sarah was a perfectly happy, well-adjusted seventeen year old, who was adopted as an infant. She always knew she was adopted, and always felt comfortable and loved in her adoptive family. Nonetheless, Sarah had a vague sense of longing -

"Sometimes I feel incomplete," Sarah told us. "I need to know more. Why did it happen? What is she like? Who is my birth father? What is he like? The older I get the more important it is to know. Its pretty frustrating being an adoptee sometimes." '

Sarah's feelings and comments are not unique and are still relevant today. For many children, who have been separated from their birth families, the sense of loss can be all pervading not just in childhood but also, and perhaps more significantly, through adulthood. Even for those children, like Sarah, who have attached to and identified strongly with their adoptive families the knowledge of being adopted and feeling loved is far from enough.

It is easy to see, with hindsight, how Sarah could have been assisted to feel more complete, her questions raise issues around the failure to promote her genetic identity, failure to make available to her full information and failure to give her access to explanation.

> ### Failure to...
>
> ♦ **Promote genetic identity**
> ♦ **Provide full explanation**
> ♦ **Give access to information**

But this rather simplistic solution in theory is, in practice, a complex process and in all probability it is the complexity factor that has disabled agencies from meeting the needs of children separated from their birth family resulting in the neglect of this fundamental aspect of their duty of care.

But the promotion of identity and addressing issues of loss and separation should not be exclusively confined to the child moving onto adoption but to *all* children who are 'looked after'. Even temporary separations from the birth family, no matter how short in terms of life time, can cause the child major difficulties in the development of their identity and healthy emotional growth.

This introduction will examine how and why agencies fail to meet the needs of children separated from their birth families, and the way in which the complexity of process can become as simplistic in application as it is in theory by adopting a new model for practice - a model that promotes identity and prepares children for life changes and their futures—

The New Life Work Model

HOW AGENCIES FAIL

The following is a true account –

*J*ean *(not her real name) was born in 1970, and she was received into 'voluntary care' when she was two months old. Jean spent the next 18 months of her life between the care of her birth mother and a number of different foster carers, and some of this time was spent in a Mother and Baby Unit. When she was two years old it was clear that rehabilitation to her birth mother was not an option and she was made subject of a Care Order.*

For the next seven years of her life Jean remained in the care system moving from placement to placement and eventually ending up in a Social Services Children's Home, where she lived for 12 months before suitable adopters were identified. Jean went to live with her adoptive parents when she was nine and a half years old and was adopted the following year. Her adopters were given copies of the Court reports for the adoption application, which gave some sketchy details of Jean's background and birth mother and a lot of information about themselves.

They were also given a hand written postcard that listed Jean's former placements.

The earliest photograph Jean has of herself is a school photo taken when she was five years old, it is not an individual photo but one taken with her class. It doesn't list her teacher or fellow pupil's names nor does it say what school it was.

Jean has no knowledge of her birth family, she doesn't know what her birth mother looks like nor does she even have a description of her. She knows her birth mother's date of birth and name. All Jean knows about her birth father is his name and ethnicity. Jean doesn't know her birth grandparents' names or who else is part of her birth family. Jean doesn't know what time of day she was born or her birth weight or whether her birth was caesarian or normal delivery. Jean has no knowledge of any genetic or hereditary disorders or health problems. In brief Jean's life before adoption is practically a blank sheet despite the fact she spent the majority of that time 'in care'.

Scary isn't it and a very uncomfortable reminder of past practice. Thankfully, and in gratitude to many enlightening research findings and the commitment of good practitioners and carers, practice has evolved and improved since Jean's experience of being in care and adoption.

But has it really evolved and improved **enough** to meet today's ever changing legislation, standards and the expanding and more complex needs of the looked after child and the child moving on to permanence?

THE NEED FOR CHANGE...

The need to change the way in which Life Work is delivered to children is based on the failings of current practice, and how and why this has happened.

Failure To Assist In The Formation And Promotion Of Identity

Identity could be described as a strange and intangible phenomenon. Difficult to define and taken for granted when we have it and yet desperately sought after when we are denied it. Its formation and existence are seldom questioned nor is its impact and influence on the life decisions we make. It could be described as a myriad of inter connecting fragments of experience and memory (one's own and other people's), anecdotal stories surrounding culture, family and life events that often preceded one's own existence.

> *It is noteworthy that during some training courses even the more experienced practitioners and carers were surprised to discover how the most obscure and trivial family information had influenced the formation of their own identities.*

Identity is not presented to us at birth but is something we gather and form along life's path, that is, providing life's path stays fairly close to the important sources of information that creates and promotes this strange and intangible phenomenon. Children separated from their birth families are not only denied access to invaluable information but also have their memories systematically discarded within the looked after system. Memories of childhood, including those of the adults involved in this stage of one's life, play a vital role in the growth of self esteem and identity formation.

Failure To Provide Information

It could be argued that in today's practice children separated from their birth families are provided with more information than ever before, and there is an element of truth within this argument. However, it is not the breadth of information provision that is lacking but the depth.

Much of the information given to children errs on the side of factual, that is systems analysis, duties of the agency, dates and so on. If these facts can be compared to the 'bare bones' then the how, what, when, where, who and why are certainly the 'meat'.

The difficulty surrounding the provision of *real* information has its roots firmly entrenched in case recording restrictions. It is not suggested that case recording should take a retrospective step but that the recording of the sort of information that assists a child's understanding and promotion of identity is dealt with creatively and separately.

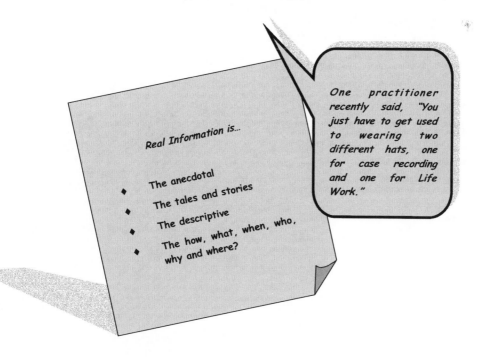

Real Information is...

• The anecdotal
• The tales and stories
• The descriptive
• The how, what, when, who, why and where?

One practitioner recently said, "You just have to get used to wearing two different hats, one for case recording and one for Life Work."

Failure To Provide Explanation

Explanation is often confused with information possibly because the questions surrounding this subject begin with the same how, what, when, where, who and why. It is indeed a sensitive area and is possibly neglected because it appears to be a daunting task with ever changing and evolving levels of interpretation.

Talking to children about what could be termed 'adult matters' creates a form of panic resulting in some practitioners and carers taking flight, and resorting to the denial of need.

It is not unusual to hear questions such as 'How can I tell them that....?' Where do I begin? When should I try to tell them that......? and so forth.

He was the product of rape and was relinquished, how do I tell him that?

She was sexually abused by her birth mother's partner, and it was likely her birth mother knew, how do I tell her that?

His birth mother gave him to a drug dealer and his wife, who were childless, to pay for her drugs habit, how do I tell him that?

She was abandoned outside a police station in the middle of winter wrapped only in a thin blanket. There was no note and no-one ever came forward, how do I tell her that?

His birth father was a schedule 1 offender but his birth mother refused to leave him, even though she knew her baby would be removed, how do I tell him that?

Her birth mother gave her 2 spiral fractures and 4 broken ribs before taking her to hospital, they found 6 more old injuries, how do I tell her that?

WHY AGENCIES FAIL

The failing of agencies to meet the needs of children separated from their birth family is not intentional but developmental. It owes much to the historical influence of legislation, social policy and abuse enquiries culminating in more structured legislation and prescriptive intervention. The focus of child protection lives within the microcosm of 'rescue from harm' and not in the macrocosm of 'lifelong protection'.

> *'The pre-occupations of the moment may assume a greater importance than other equally significant matters that remain in comparative obscurity'. (HMSO, 1991).*

The concentrated interest in legal proceedings and the making of an order has diluted and, in some cases, eroded innovative freedom and creative initiative in some aspects of the planning for children's futures.

The corporate parenting model introduced by 'Quality Protects' **(DoH, 1998)** did, in many ways, exacerbate the failings of agencies to meet certain areas of need for children separated from their birth family, the very counter objective to its aim. The purpose of Quality Protects in improving the delivery of services to children gave recognition to the shortfall in the provision of information about the child's looked after experience. Consequently 'Looked After Children' (LAC) documentation was introduced as a solution.

Whilst the corporate parenting model is functional and meets statutory requirements, LAC documentation itself fails to provide *real* information as it deals in the factual which identifies the child but fails to promote the child's identity.

The introduction of LAC gave birth to complacency, with agencies being satisfied that if LAC documentation was complete then so too was the information a child needed. Not so, it is not just having the knowledge about one's date of birth that develops the embryo of identity formation but it is the circumstances surrounding one's birth that begins this process. Circumstances such as the time, the day, the delivery, what happened, when and where and who, even the weather, the list is endless. This principal needs to be applied to **all the facts** about a child's life, something LAC documentation is unable to provide.

LAC documentation...

♦ Gives factual information

♦ Identifies the child but falls short of promoting the child's identity

♦ Leads agencies to be complacent about their duty to provide information

♦ Is not a source of *real* information

LAC documentation should be perceived for what it is, a catalogue of data and not an information source.

LAC had yet another negative impact on the ability of agencies to meet the needs of children. It generated a proliferation of paperwork and, combined with the growth of complexity in caseloads, resulted in already overworked practitioners having no time to address areas of failing outside of the child protection arena. Promotion of identity and preparation for life changes for children had fallen off the league table of 'things to do' and the deficiencies were being systematically squeezed into obscurity.

THINGS TO DO TODAY... ✓

- 3 Child protection visits
- Conference report
- Statement of evidence
- LAC docs for 'A'
- 2 Summaries
- Organise contact for 'C'
- Cover duty from 2pm
- Visit 'B' after school
- Evening boarding out visit

The solution was thought to be found in the provision of 'Life Story Books' for children separated from birth families and moving on to permanence, not least because the Courts were taking a more proactive role in practice stipulation and making Life Story Books a prerequisite in final care plans.

Whilst the Life Story Book approach did fill a significant void in addressing the needs of children separated from birth family it no longer *fully* meets the needs of children and this is evidenced in its failings.

HOW THE 'LIFE STORY BOOK' APPROACH FAILS

It would be unjust and unfair to denigrate this approach without acknowledging the benefits it has given to many children who, but for its existence, would have been denied any form of information. The approach has also introduced some pioneering techniques for working with children and assisting them in their understanding of perplexing concepts and situations, that are still relevant today.

LIFE WORK - WHAT MODEL?

Furthermore it has been, up to now, the *only* 'model' for practice in the areas of identity promotion, information, explanation and preparation. Its singularity has not been confined to the UK.

Despite the major social and economic changes in Europe over the last few decades and the subsequent workshops created to share knowledge and experience of key issues encompassing best practice for children, there was no other definitive model. **Exchanging Visions (BAAF 1998).**

1st FAILING

The first failing of the 'Life Story Book' approach is its over simplification of the process of promoting identity, dealing with loss and separation and preparation for moving on by making one book the central and only point of reference. In addition to this the book being referred to as a 'story book' undervalues this important work with children, (is it true or just a tale?), work that should be more appropriately called 'Life Work'.

2nd FAILING

The Life Story Book approach confuses the need for information with the need for therapeutic work. Ryan and Walker (1985) state that the completion of Life Story Books should not be used as a vehicle to undertake therapeutic work with children, and yet by its own participatory mode it encourages this dual approach. It is generally accepted that completing a Life Story Book with a child is a means to assisting them to explore issues and make sense of life events as they are revealed in the process. Testimony to this is the frequency of which the question 'Do they have a Life Story Book?' is asked when children are displaying symptomatic behaviours of confusion, loss and separation.

3rd FAILING

The approach relies heavily on the task centred model of intervention being a one off piece of work that is invariably begun to coincide with the submission of the final care plan to the Court. In some cases the task is done on the 'hurry up' and there is little if any quality control. The task is frequently the responsibility of the willing sole worker, possibly the one with the most available time, whether or not this person has the knowledge, skills or experience to undertake this important work. The expectation that one person is proficient in all the areas associated with Life Work is unrealistic and naive, and is it really fair to children that the quality of their Life Work is dependant on whether or not the person undertaking the work is creative or not, enjoys it or not, or has or has not the knowledge or experience?

4th FAILING

The approach relies on the participation of the child to the exclusion of the unwilling and unable. How often is the question raised 'Do they have a Life Story Book? And answered with 'No, they didn't want to take part' or 'They are too young to understand'.

5th FAILING

The task of compiling a Life Story Book is usually set outside the framework of the care planning process and therefore lacks structural direction in terms of time scales that are in tune with a child's changing needs. This factor, when linked with the participatory nature of the approach, isolates the task even further away from the care planning process.

6th FAILING

The approach has the potential to deny the promotion of a child's identity by focusing on their looked after experience and becoming an informal extension of LAC documentation. It also has the potential to fail to preserve the anecdotal, minutia and hearsay essential to identity promotion. The contemporaneous recording of this information helps to ensure its accuracy, Life Story Books are usually compiled in retrospect.

7th FAILING

'Life Story Books' are predominantly associated with the child who is moving on to permanence, and in the main, adoption. Not every looked after child is afforded the same level of assistance regardless of the fact that *all* looked after children are children separated from their birth family.

8th FAILING

The approach fails by confining its concentration to the child alone. Children do not exist in isolation and yet the work to promote identity, address issues of loss and separation and preparation usually detaches the child from their environment and the adults who are responsible for their day to day care needs. Preparation for a child's life changes can only be successful if all the people involved in the child's life are prepared for the life changes this will bring to them. The needs of the child's primary carers must be addressed in order for them in turn to meet the needs of the child. Furthermore the child's carers and network play a crucial role in the recording of *real* information but despite this many carers are denied the opportunity to participate.

9th FAILING

The final failing, and in many respects one of the most significant, is the 'Life Story Book' approach's lack of success in encouraging birth families to participate. In all probability there are numerous factors that contribute to this and there will always be some birth families that are unable and/or unwilling to co-operate, no matter what inducement is offered to them. Given that birth families and their networks are the most significant source of genetic information the disregarding of this failing is inexcusable.

THE NEED FOR CHANGE

*I*n order to promote identity and prepare children who are separated from their birth families for their futures the 'Life Story Book' approach must be set aside and the alternative, The New Life Work Model be promoted. This model is the first definitive model for practice.

The New Life Work Model differs greatly to its predecessor, the Life Story Book approach, in relation to its application but they share a common theoretical base.

> *'There is nothing so practical as a good theory.' (Bowlby.1988)*

This was remarked to John Bowlby, and it is most certainly true in the case of promoting children's identity and preparation for their futures.

The primary aim of Life Work has to and must be designed to meet the *lifelong* needs of children separated from their birth families. The promotion and maintenance of a child's genetic identity and positive image of themselves and their birth families is pivotal to achieving this aim.

Life Work should pay attention to the stigmatisation of the looked after child and the additional burdens they carry as researched and concluded by Nash **(1973)**.

Life Work should set out to avoid the problems that could occur later in life that are directly related to the issue of low self esteem. Hoghughi **(1978)** identified the problems for the looked after child linking them to low self esteem.

It is so often the case that in the early stages of permanence placement the emphasis is placed on the development of attachments to and identification with the new permanent family. In the order of things this is probably a very positive goal to aim for as all practitioners and carers want children to 'settle' in their new family. However, this invariably takes precedence over the promotion of genetic identity despite research findings that clearly indicate the need to address issues of identity, separation and loss in order to assist in the transfer of attachments:

> *'A child cannot transfer attachments and therefore move on to permanency unless issues of identity then loss and separation are addressed.' (Fahlberg, 1994).*

For babies and infants the promotion of genetic identity is at risk of being less and less significant, and being pushed into obscurity, as the child grows more and more attached to and identifies with their adoptive family.

The denial of genetic identity can not only lead to a sense of being incomplete but can also have more serious consequences.

'It is difficult to grow up as a psychologically healthy adult if denied access to one's own history.' (Fahlberg, 1994).

Life Work must **competently** and **qualitatively** address issues of loss and separation. Grief has a paralysing effect on functioning at any age but for children it is pernicious.

'Of course, the pain of separation from those we love is for all of us a devastating experience, but for the dependant child the whole of his or her world collapses and everything loses meaning.' (Winnicott, 1986).

Life Work should offer opportunities for children to grieve appropriately.

'When a person is unable to complete a mourning task in child-hood he either has to surrender his emotions in order that they do not suddenly overwhelm him or else he may be haunted con-stantly throughout his life with a sadness for which he can never find an appropriate explanation.' (Schoenberg et al., 1970).

LIFE WORK SHOULD...

In the light of the many research findings in respect of the needs of children, who are separated from their families of birth, it is evident as to what Life Work should achieve.

- Play a significant role in the promotion of identity.

- Offer children a positive image of their birth family.

- Encourage the elevation of a child's self esteem.

- Give children information and explanation.

- Take an holistic view of the child's needs and the needs of others involved in their life.

- Empower those entrusted with the care of children to identify and continue their Life Work needs throughout their life.

- Be a priority in the care of children separated from their birth family.

- Be a quality service for *all* children separated from their birth family.

The New Life Work model sets out to meet these requirements by having a multi dimensional approach, which is an integral part of the care planning process, separated only by task but incorporated by aim. It encourages inter agency and professional collaboration.

It does not primarily focus on the child, although the paramouncy of the child's welfare drives the process. It has a breadth of focus that includes all the significant adults in the child's life, including the birth family, to assist in the process and offer the child lifelong protection. The model does not depend on the child's participation and therefore it meets the needs of *all* looked after children, irrespective of their age, cognitive ability, willingness, status or care plan.

It begins from the looked after child's first statutory review (or earlier depending on circumstances) and a significant part of the preparatory work is done *for* the child as opposed to *with* the child, in that the provision of *real* information is made available whether or not the child is willing or able to take part at that time.

HOW THE NEW LIFE WORK MODEL OPERATES

Preserving Children's 'Looked After' Memories

This is the start of *real* information for the child and it is achieved by the provision of My Memory Books, *(Nicholls, 2005 b)* Photo Albums and Memory Boxes. The child owns the books, albums and boxes, and wherever the child lives so too do their books and boxes. Thus ensuring that although the child may not be *permanently* separated from their birth family the part of their life when they were has not left a gap in their memory, or the memory of their birth family.

Preparing The Child And Adults For Life Changes And/Or Permanency

As the model is an integral part of the care planning process it allows early identification of the need for direct work or referral for specialised therapeutic work. The model provides material to assist primary carers and professionals to undertake the work. This component of the model also deals with the wishes and feelings of the child during this process and ways in which they can be recorded for the child in later life.

In the new model preparation for moving on is not confined to the child but extends to their temporary carer also, acknowledging their sense of loss and assisting them to come to terms with the life changes that come when a child moves on.

Promoting Identity

The process of identity formation and its promotion will have already begun via the child's Memory Books. However, the Memory Books alone would not provide the sort of information that would fully promote genetic identity and positive images of the birth family. In order for the model to achieve this goal it provides a comprehensive Family History Book that records as much information as possible about the birth family tree, birth family members, family origins, cultural and ethnic history and a wealth of family stories from the factual to the rumour. The model offers advice on how to create a Family History Book.

The model also acknowledges the key role of temporary primary carers in working with *all* children separated from their birth family and not just those moving onto adoption. It offers methods and techniques, from a clear theoretical base, for temporary carers to promote identity and build self-esteem. It helps carers develop ways to assist the child's understanding and avoid attachment confusion.

Providing Explanation

The New Life Work model recognises the difficulties many adults have with explanation. As stated earlier this is a very sensitive area, and whilst professionals may be qualified to perform this task, it is far more likely that it would be the child's primary carers, adopters and/or permanent carers that the child seeks explanation from (the latter two especially so, as the child develops and demands more mature answers to their questions) . The model guides carers and adopters through the process of explanation, giving them opportunities to bring to the child positive images of their birth family, ways to combat the negativity associated with being looked after and reduce the debilitating blame factor.

But the model also recognises that explanation does not necessarily come in the form of answering questions.

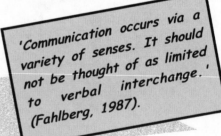

'Communication occurs via a variety of senses. It should not be thought of as limited to verbal interchange.' (Fahlberg, 1987).

It not only addresses the fears of adults around this issue but also helps build their confidence in their innate skills in communicating with children. This is achieved by the provision of training and development courses and additional material that offers a variety of methods and suggestions to assist.

The New Life Work Model's Integration With The Care Planning Process

Responsibility for the instigation and facilitation of the stages and processes of the model should be assigned to the Adoption and Fostering Service of agencies such as local authorities. There are a number of reasons for this, the more obvious are set out below:

• The completion of Life Work has historically failed when set within the parameters of child protection work or care proceedings. This is not, in any way, a criticism of child protection social workers. It is, in fact, an acknowledgment that the complexities of child protection casework cannot accommodate any form of additional duties, particularly any duties that in terms of prioritisation would, at certain times, have to be set aside. By the same token delegating responsibility to Adoption and Fostering Services is not suggesting social workers in this arena have more time to devote to Life Work but that, in terms of prioritisation, it is less likely to be set aside.

PRIORITISATION

CONFLICT OF INTEREST

• There is another fundamental reason for removing overall responsibility for Life Work from the child protection sector which is the potential for conflict of interest. A substantial part of the New Life Work Model requires the participation and co-operation of the birth family and this might be more difficult for the child protection social worker to achieve having been involved in the care proceedings.

25

- Life Work, and particularly the components of this New Life Work model, are traditionally an area of expertise within Adoption and Fostering Services, and it is the Adoption and Fostering Service that assesses and recommends the approval of foster carers and adopters.

> **ASSESS AND APPROVE CARERS AND ADOPTERS**

- The process of assessment and approval makes a requirement on Adoption and Fostering Services to provide a continuing and comprehensive training and development programme. Training and development in relation to the model would be more easily assigned to existing programmes.

> **TRAINING**

- The Adoption and Fostering Services have more direct and frequent links with foster carers and adopters.

> **DIRECT AND FREQUENT LINKS**

- The Adoption and Fostering Services are responsible for driving the adoption process within the care planning process.

> **DRIVE THE ADOPTION PROCESS**

'We believe that a Life Book should be started for each child at the time he first comes into care.' Fahlberg, 1994.

The New Life Work model begins the process of Life Work from the looked after child's first statutory review, which is four weeks from the start of their looked after experience. *In some cases it begins earlier if the prognosis for re-unification is poor or it is known that the assessment process will be protracted.*

At the child's four month review there is a requirement for the decision for permanence to be defined. Permanence could be rehabilitation to their birth family, twin track planning, concurrent planning, adoption, permanence via fostering, special guardianship etc. At this stage a Life Work planning meeting would be co-ordinated. Members of the Life Work planning group would be decided upon via consultation between the child's social worker, foster carer and the Adoption and Fostering Service, and should reflect the child's already identified needs.

REMIT...

* Identify Life Work needs √
* Allocate tasks √
* Timetabling √
* Quality √
* Share responsibility √

The remit of the Life Work planning group is to identify the child's Life Work needs which includes quality control. Membership would be fluid and encourage inter-agency collaboration and promote corporate team responsibility. The frequency of subsequent Life Work planning meetings is decided by the group and is dependent on the child's needs, progress and definition of the child's care plan and the needs of individual members to consult with the group.

The Life Work planning group will play a significant role in the formulation of support plans and the identification of the life long needs of the child and how these can be met.

The model also allows for additional Life Work methodology to be 'bolted on' to its framework to enhance it in terms of Life Appreciation Days and Later Life Letters.

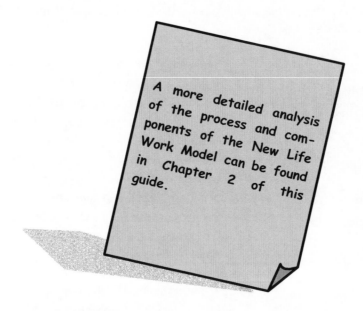

It is worth remembering that in relation to Life Work there is no such thing as *too much* information!

The Life Work planning group will decide on and facilitate these two extra components of the model.

A more detailed analysis of the process and components of the New Life Work Model can be found in Chapter 2 of this guide.

THE ROLE OF TEMPORARY PRIMARY CARERS WITHIN THE NEW LIFE WORK MODEL

It is evident from the process previously described that primary carers (in both foster and residential care) play a key role within the new model. Throughout the process of the model their participation and contribution is vital and this is emphasised by their mandatory and permanent membership of the Life Work planning group.

But the primary carers' role would not be confined to discussion and consultation only. There would be an expectation, given their relationship to the child and their care needs, that they play a major part in helping to promote the child's identity and in assisting the child to come to terms with the separation from their birth family.

The model not only acknowledges the skills of temporary carers, and uses them to good effect, it also addresses carers' own needs when preparing children for permanency.

Training that accompanies the model will offer primary carers and professionals methods and techniques to enhance and develop their skills in communicating and working with children to promote identity, deal with issues of separation and loss and how to give children meaningful explanation. See page 197 of this guide for further details.

How Primary Carers Can Promote Identity

Primary carers have an unparalleled advantage within the Life Work process by virtue of their place in a looked after child's life.

They hold a position of trust and have wide-ranging opportunities of spontaneity for explaining and informing that other professionals can only dream of. Earlier in this introduction it was suggested that the complexity of the Life Work process can become as simplistic in application as it is in theory, and it is the simplistic approach that supports the primary carers' role, employing the fundamental base of honesty and trust.

Children separated from their birth families need honest information about and explanation for their life changes immediately the separation takes place, and who better to explain this than the person who is nurturing them.

It should never be assumed that children understand why they are looked after or even what a foster or residential carer is or does. This is the starting point in developing trust, understanding and opening doors of opportunity to promote identity and preparing children for future life changes.   As it is the child's primary carer who is most likely to offer this sort of explanation it is they who begin the process of trust. To the child their primary temporary carers are the link to their past and the bridge to their futures.

If, from the child's perspective, the link appears weak and the bridge only under construction the subsequent confusion can disable both the carer and the child from moving on.

Information and explanation are two of the key factors in avoiding confusion. Once the child has an understanding of the role of their temporary carer then reasons for them being looked after need to be clarified.

No easy task, particularly for the carer who is looking after the abused child, when one of the fundamental aspects of promoting identity is being positive about the child's history and birth family. However, developing an understanding of the parenting role is an excellent starting point.

By using Fahlberg's three part parenting model **(Fahlberg, 1994)** children can begin to understand what is expected of parents, which then leads to explanations as to why some parents, and, therefore, the child's parents, are unable to look after their children.

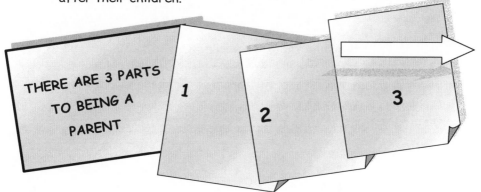

THERE ARE 3 PARTS TO BEING A PARENT

1

2

3

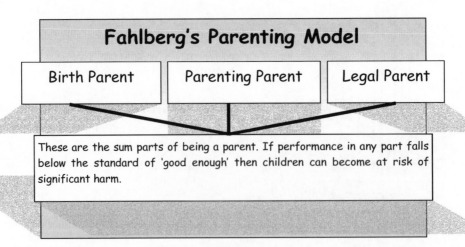

As with many good theories the model is simple to follow, the wording can be adapted for any age group, it allows for creativity in presentation and can be tailored to the individual child. It is best presented in a visual form and the carer can decide which method of presentation suits the child. There are no rules as to how it should be presented and explained, thus allowing the carer to use the method that they feel most comfortable with.

Fahlberg explains that parenting is made up of three parts, Birth Parent, Parenting Parent and Legal Parent. Within each part there are a number of tasks parents have to undertake.

Explaining to the child the birth parent part of parenting and what birth parents actually give to them is an ideal vehicle to build self esteem, start the process of genetic identity promotion and enable the child to have a positive image of their parents.

Moving on to the parenting parent, the part that gives care and protection, helps the child to understand just how difficult this task can be and sets the scene for the reasons why some parents are unable to perform this part of parenting. It is also a good opportunity to re-emphasise the role of temporary carers and their task of offering care and protection whilst decisions are made for the child's future.

Once the child has a good understanding of the parenting role and its identified tasks, an explanation as to why they are unable to live with their birth family becomes less arduous. It will enable the carer to explain more easily without laying blame or leading the child to believe they are the root cause, even for those children who have been abused or relinquished. However, it is essential that the role of agencies and their statutory duties to protect are clarified for the child.

Finally, an explanation of the legal parenting part will help the child understand the who, what, how and why decisions are made. It is also a chance to explain the legal processes that are taking place and the duties of the agency.

Explaining the 3 part parenting model to children can get a bit muddled, it needs to be transformed to:

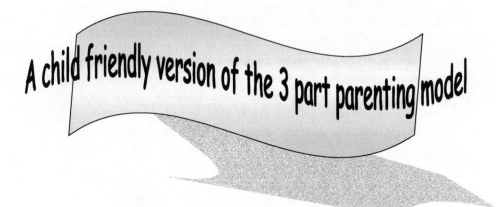

A child friendly version of the 3 part parenting model

The child friendly version of the 3 part parenting model can be found in Chapter 4 of this guide.

Using the Fahlberg model in helping the child's understanding of parenting is not only invaluable in its purest sense but provides a wealth of opportunities for the child to explore and express their own feelings about their sense of loss and separation, and for the carer to exhibit a positive view of their birth family. It provides advantageous moments for the carer to talk with the child about the positives associated with their family, history, and culture, all of which are important ingredients of identity promotion. The links to the child's past will be strengthened and the bridge to their future more visibly constructed.

The explanation process can again be tailored to suit the individual child's ability, age and level of understanding, and again using a variety of techniques and methods that are acceptable to the carer also.

More in depth explanation comes in the form of *'reasons why'* linked mainly to the task of the parenting parent. Throughout this process reference to the fact that inability to perform the parenting parent role may not be a conscious failing but a consequence of a set or sets of circumstance and history. It is here that the carer can remove or diminish the negativity attached to parents who fail to care and protect yet another aspect of identity promotion and the building of self-esteem.

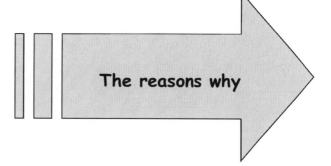

The reasons why

The 'reasons why' fall into five clear 'umbrella' categories and they are:

 **1**

> Their parents may have problems and troubles of their own that it makes it really difficult for them to care for others and do all the tasks of the parenting parent.

 **2**

> Their parents may never have been taught how to look after and care for others.

 **3**

> Their parents may be too ill to care for others.

 **4**

> Their parents may not be able to learn how to be a parenting parent.

 **5**

> Their parents may have been shown the wrong way to look after children.

For some children the reasons for separation may fall within more than one category and care should be taken that the primary category is clarified.

The temptation to fit every explanation into the category of '*too ill*' must be avoided, for example drug use, alcoholism etc should primarily come within category one. It is likely in some cases that category one leads to the secondary reason of being '*too ill*' and this should be clarified.

Far too many times, in the past, children have been told they are unable to live with their birth parents because their parents are ill. This can give the child unrealistic expectations that their parent will be restored to good health within a time-scale that they understand, this is misleading and dishonest.

The Fahlberg 3 part parenting model is used frequently within the New Life Work Model and its supporting material such as 'What Does Adopted Mean? - A Young Child's Guide to Adoption.' *(Nicholls, 2005a).*

The process of explanation relies heavily on honesty with the proviso of age appropriate language and interpretation and it should lay the foundation for a more detailed analysis as the child matures.

IN CONCLUSION

The promotion of identity and the preparation of children, who are separated from their birth families, for their futures is crucial to their life long needs and emotional security.

Over the last three decades social policy and legislation have sought to improve services to children and whilst children in the looked after system today receive a better standard of service than their predecessors the bureaucratic systems still fail some of their most fundamental needs.

The failings are not intentional but owe more to a lack of creative and innovative developments in the field of Life Work. Life work has become 'stuck' in outdated methodology that has dislodged itself from the theoretical base that underpins this important aspect of the duty of care to *all* looked after children.

Life Work, with all its complexities and necessities, has been reduced to the provision of a solitary Life Story Book. The production of a Life Story Book depends on a child's ability and willingness to participate to the exclusion of the unwilling and the unable. Furthermore it has become a more informal extension of LAC documentation, the implementation of which has done much to deny the child the sort of information essential to the promotion of identity and preservation of memory.

The New Life Work Model has a breadth of focus that promotes identity and prepares children for their futures in an innovative, creative and individualistic approach that is lacking in the Life Story Book approach. Its integration with the care planning process, inter agency and professional collaboration converts the complexities of Life Work to simplistic application.

It recognises and acknowledges the skills and key role of temporary primary carers and offers methods and techniques, within a clearly defined theoretical framework, to assist them to promote identity and help children understand the reasons why they are unable to live with their birth families.

Its corporate team approach with shared responsibility for its process and completion is more likely to be successful in providing a quality service to the child separated from their birth family.

The New Life Work Model

The Differences

THE LIFE STORY BOOK APPROACH

- Is usually only for children moving on to permanence
- Usually begins at the end of being looked after
- Is a one off task for one worker
- Confuses the need for information with therapy
- Excludes the unwilling or unable child
- Excludes birth family
- Doesn't identify lifelong Life Work needs

THE NEW LIFE WORK MODEL

- Is for *all* children separated from birth family
- Begins early in a child's looked after experience
- Is part of the care planning process and encourages shared responsibility
- Identifies, clarifies and separates therapeutic needs
- Is not reliant on the child's participation
- Encourages inclusion of birth families
- Identifies lifelong Life Work needs

CHAPTER 2

THE PROCESS AND COMPONENTS OF THE MODEL

CARE PLANNING OR PLANNING WITH CARE?

Does Care Planning Really Mean Planning With Care?

We are all familiar with the process of care planning, after all its structure and clearly defined stages leaves nothing to chance, it prevents 'drift', offers guidelines on what to do next and gives us structural comfort.

So how is it that this clearly defined structure of process has resulted in the neglect of Life Work, one of the most fundamental aspects of care for the child separated from their birth family?

Answer: Because Life Work has been excluded from the process of care planning and dealt with in isolation thus questioning if we really are planning with care. This new model for practice brings Life Work seamlessly into the care planning process.

CARE PLANNING PROCESS

NEW LIFE WORK MODEL

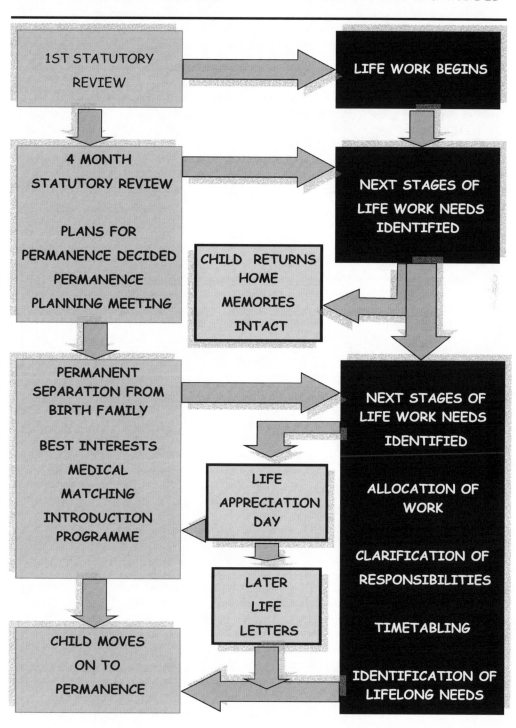

Life Work begins with the provision of age appropriate Memory Books, Memory Boxes and the start of Photograph Albums. These should be given to the child's primary carer who has overall responsibility for the preservation of the child's 'looked after' memories. For children of an age and understanding the process of explanation and information should have been started earlier than this review, however the provision of the Memory Books will assist carers and professionals to further develop a child's understanding.

This process should begin earlier than the 1st review in cases whereby the prognosis for reunification is poor and/ or it is likely that the assessment process will be protracted.

The next stage of Life Work planning now gets underway whatever the review decision. If it is a clear decision of reunification then preparing the child, and their primary carer, for moving on should be put in place immediately.

Planning the child's Life Work needs should continue within twin track planning and concurrent placements although some elements would not be addressed until end of assessments and conclusion of proceedings. Those taking responsibility for the Life Work could link into permanence planning meetings at this stage. It is here that therapeutic needs should begin to be identified.

Whilst not appropriate to begin interviews for the Family History Book prior to final proceedings it would be worthwhile to consider what work for the book could be addressed now.

As final proceedings approach and the plan for the child's future is clearer it might be helpful to set up a Life Work Planning Group to identify who will be responsible for what aspects of the child's next stage of Life Work needs and begin timetabling the work to be done.

The preparation work comes to the fore at this stage and assisting the child's primary carer to move on will be invaluable particularly when introduction programmes are set in motion.

Probably the most significant piece of work in the final stages is the Family History Book. It may be that this will not be completed in time for the child to take possession of it before moving on for a variety of reasons which are dealt with later in this section. However, care should be taken not to let its completion drift and it could be that the Life Work Planning Group may need to meet after the child has been placed permanently.

The Family History book is vital to identity promotion.

COMMENTS ABOUT PROCESS, IMPLEMENTATION AND WORDING

The process of the New Life Work Model is not intended to be rigidly prescriptive and agencies need to modify or adapt the model accordingly in order to be compatible with the available resources within the agency. The flow chart of how the model integrates with the care planning process is the optimum or ideal. The only really prescriptive part of the model is the operation and timing of its main components, how this is achieved is the decision of the agency.

Each of the *main* components serves a specific task to fully meet a child's Life Work needs and are, therefore, essential. The *secondary* components enhance those needs and are, therefore, desirable.

If agencies would like advice about implementing the New Life Work Model the author is available to assist (see page 197 of this guide).

The words used to describe certain components of the model can be modified to agency preferences e.g Life Appreciation Days—some agencies prefer to call this aspect of Life Work 'Celebration Days'.

LIFE WORK NEED   MET BY

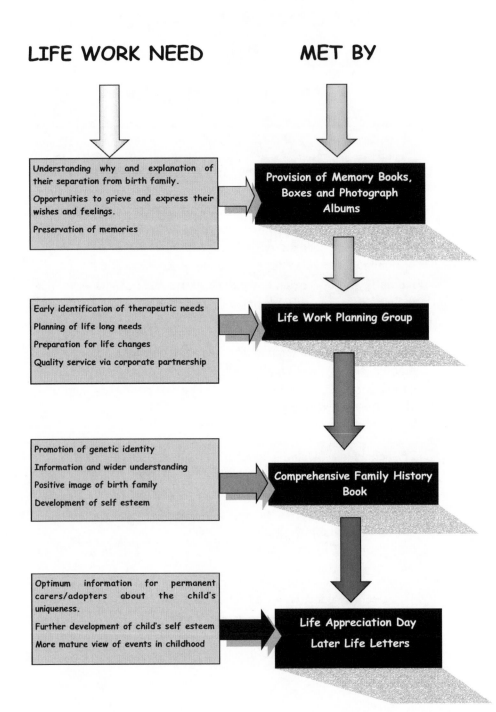

Understanding why and explanation of their separation from birth family.

Opportunities to grieve and express their wishes and feelings.

Preservation of memories

Provision of Memory Books, Boxes and Photograph Albums

Early identification of therapeutic needs

Planning of life long needs

Preparation for life changes

Quality service via corporate partnership

Life Work Planning Group

Promotion of genetic identity

Information and wider understanding

Positive image of birth family

Development of self esteem

Comprehensive Family History Book

Optimum information for permanent carers/adopters about the child's uniqueness.

Further development of child's self esteem

More mature view of events in childhood

Life Appreciation Day
Later Life Letters

THE COMPONENTS OF THE MODEL

The Model has 4 core and 2 secondary components

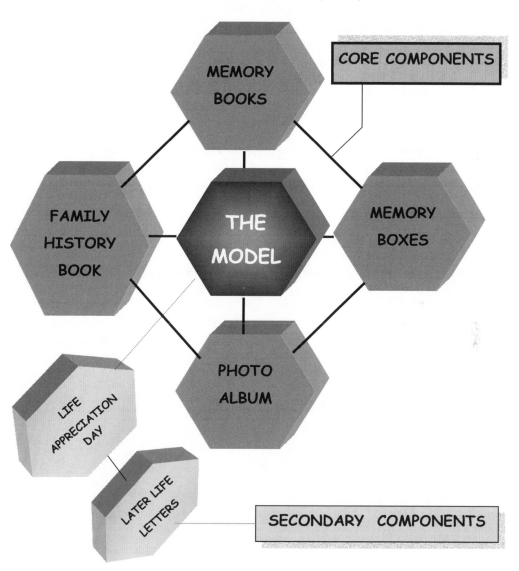

Keeping Copies

Preserving the work completed within the New Life Work Model is worth serious consideration. All the material belongs to the child and should be wherever the child is. There is no doubt that new families will do everything they can to preserve the material but, in a child and adolescent's life, possessions do get lost or destroyed.

Certainly the Family History Book should be copied by either photo copy or scanning and preserved on disc, and the fact that a copy exists should be made known to the child and their family. If the book is compiled with a pc keeping copies would be no difficult task by copying to disc and storage would not be a problem, discs take up very little room in a child's file.

A copy of the Family History Book should be given to the birth family with any identifying factors about their new family deleted if it is inappropriate for the birth family to know.

Some foster carers have expressed concern about the child who would destroy their Memory Book in times of anger or sadness. If a foster carer believes this to be a probability then they should photocopy as they go along, using the agency's resources, of course.

Unfortunately Memory Boxes cannot be duplicated but keeping an itinerary of their contents and the significance of the objects is better than nothing. This can also be stored on a child's file.

Scanning photo albums and saving to disc would also be helpful.

CORE COMPONENT 1 -
Memory Books

The primary purpose of Memory Books is to record a child's experiences whilst separated from their birth family and during the time when assessments and decisions about their future are being made. They not only record a child's memories but also offer an explanation as to why the child is separated from their birth family and assist the child in understanding what processes are taking place to decide on their long term future.

Memory Books should begin as early as possible in that period. Children should have a new Memory Book for each new **temporary** placement because Memory Books relate to temporary placements.

When a child moves onto permanence via adoption their adoptive parents can continue preserving life memories in whatever form they and the child prefer.

When a child moves onto permanence via fostering, including long term arrangements, the recording of their day to day life whilst separated from their birth family should continue. Permanent carers can either use additional Memory Books appropriate to the child's age or create other forms of recording memories.

The ultimate responsibility for the completion of Memory Books lies with the child's primary carer. If a child is unable or unwilling to approach a Memory Book then their carer should complete it for them to ensure none of the child's memories are lost whatever the decision is for their future.

Other professionals involved in the child's life can complete sections of the book also. Certainly the child's social worker should assist in the sections about reasons for the child's separation from their birth family. Whoever facilitates and supervises contact can assist in the completion of the contact diary sections. Then, of course there is the birth family who should be encouraged to help in the completion of the book.

The birth family are more likely to co-operate in this stage of Life Work as Memory Books are not an indication of permanent separation plans but a way to record looked after memories. It is also an opportunity for the birth families to gain a more comprehensive picture of their child's life at that time by reading other sections in the book as they are completed.

A RISK FACTOR NOTE

- *When there are risks attached to the birth family having knowledge of the child's whereabouts or placement details the Memory Book should not be shown to the birth family.*

- *They can still assist in its completion by professionals making notes of their comments and any relevant information they give to be entered in the Memory Book outside of their presence.*

There are currently 3 different types of 'My Memory Books' available:-

Babies and Toddlers

Age 4+

Age 8+

They vary in their design, layout, language and content significance according to the child's age.   The 8+ Memory Book, in some circumstances, could be appropriate for children over 12 and young adolescents.

In the books age 4+ and 8+ there are sections that encourage the child to reveal their feelings, record their thoughts and wishes and to assist the primary carer to understand the child's wants and understanding of their situation. Some of the sections are designed to help the child's primary carer to give explanations in age appropriate terms.

This is not only an explanation about why they are separated from their birth family but also about the role of their primary carer.

- Memory Books are to record a child's looked after experience and are for children in temporary care.

- The books are sectioned according to areas of the child's life e.g friends, family, contact, wishes and feelings etc.

- They are 'dip in' books and memories are added gradually as they happen.

- The 4+ and 8+ Memory Books begin with the section 'All About Me' to generate the child's interest in the book.

- The books are non-denominational and are suitable for children of all ethnicities, culture and beliefs. Nor are they discriminatory and there are images of children with disabilities.

- Sections are complimented with relevant clip art and children's poetry.

- The books are not gender specific and are suitable for both girls and boys.

Understanding their primary carers' role is particularly relevant for children in foster care, as when living within an alternative family can generate confusion for a child in terms of the long term plans for their future.

Each Memory Book has its own set of guidelines on how to complete the books, what sort of information should be recorded and what should not. There are really no hard and fast rules about completing Memory Books although there are a couple of golden ones ...

1. There can never be too much information
2. The anecdotal should take precedence over the factual.

Memory Books are the property of the child and wherever the child goes so too do their books. When a child is reunited with their birth family they take their books home with them thus ensuring there are no memory gaps in their life. *(See also page 48—Keeping Copies).*

CORE COMPONENT 2 -
Memory Boxes

Memory Boxes should be bright and colourful, suit the age of the child and reflect their particular interests. They can be bought or custom made and decorated. They are to preserve *tangible* memories, items that would not fit into a book.

Examples could be-

♦ Any form of school certificates, reports, programmes for concerts

♦ End of term school work, school books, project work

♦ Ticket stubs from the cinema, theatre, bowling etc

♦ Restaurant receipts

♦ Birth tags, hospital tags

♦ Removed stitches, milk teeth, locks of hair from hair cuts

♦ Favourite and outgrown toys, teddies, books

♦ Drawings, notes, letters

♦ Holiday receipts, leaflets, events programmes

♦ First shoes or other significant clothing

♦ Anything to do with contact to their birth family

And so the list goes on.

Items should be labelled with dates and the significance of their memories. There could be boxes within boxes, such as a box for small toys with a book explaining why they were significant, or a contact box. There could be colourful ring binders with card pages for small items to be pasted on and enough room for dates and explanation.

Anyone can contribute to a child's Memory Box not just the carers and the child. Think about the person who supervises contact and what they could contribute, or wider family of the carers, even school friends, group leaders etc. There should be no limit to the number of Memory Boxes a child owns and they need to be treasure troves of memories.

Nothing is unimportant!

CORE COMPONENT 3 -

Photograph Albums

Temporary carers of looked after children are no strangers to the camera, especially foster carers who invariably take hundreds of photos of the child. There are times when the child doesn't actually take possession of these photos when moving on.

Many carers fear that the photos will get lost or be discarded and they keep them in order to preserve them. Although 'backtracking' for photos often results in carers sifting out the numerous images, this is not really a satisfactory way of providing a visual record of the child's looked after experience.

Within the New Life Work Model photograph albums are as significant as the Memory Books and Boxes. Carers are encouraged to see albums for what they really should be- that is, a photographic journal. Whilst images of the child are essential, carers are asked to think beyond just photos of the child and include photos of places, the home, the child's bed-

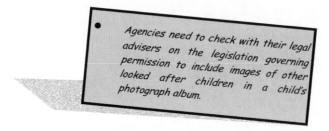

Agencies need to check with their legal advisers on the legislation governing permission to include images of other looked after children in a child's photograph album.

room, people who have been part of the child's life whilst living with them, their nursery, school, favourite shops, friends, neighbours, the family car and so on.

Shop bought albums are fine providing there is space for text to explain the image, the who, what and where. Some carers may be happy to make their own albums so they can be more creative with the displays. Agencies should be prepared to meet the costs of films, processing and duplicate photos and, in some cases, even the camera or provide access to a scanner.

Photographs should include ordinary day to day happenings as well as special occasions. Labelling of photos can make reference to the text or a page in the child's Memory Book e.g

"This is a picture of you all dressed up in your new clothes ready to go to the wedding as we talked about in Events and Happenings in your Memory Book".

"This is the shop we stopped at on our way home from school, you always wanted a packet of cheese and onion crisps".

"This is Mr.Jones the butcher, we used to buy your favourite sausages from him and he always called you his favourite customer".

Labelling photographs can offer additional information, stories and memories that are not in another part of the Memory Book.

MY PHOTO ALBUM

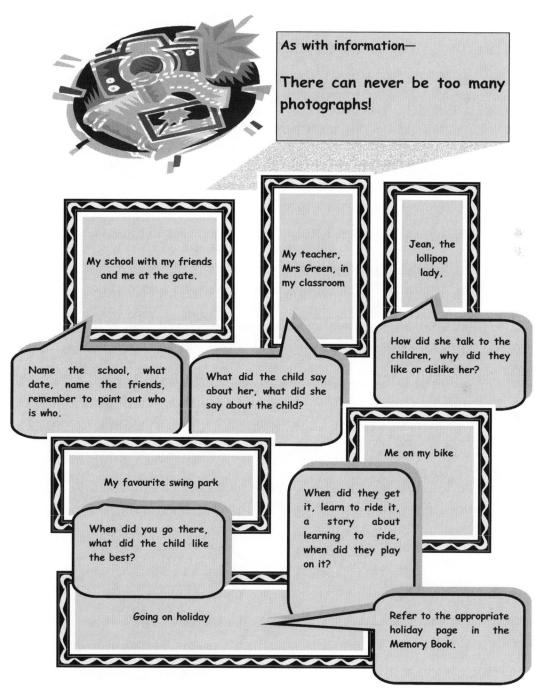

As with information—

There can never be too many photographs!

My school with my friends and me at the gate.

My teacher, Mrs Green, in my classroom

Jean, the lollipop lady,

How did she talk to the children, why did they like or dislike her?

Name the school, what date, name the friends, remember to point out who is who.

What did the child say about her, what did she say about the child?

My favourite swing park

Me on my bike

When did they get it, learn to ride it, a story about learning to ride, when did they play on it?

When did you go there, what did the child like the best?

Going on holiday

Refer to the appropriate holiday page in the Memory Book.

CORE COMPONENT 4 -
Family History Books

For children who are permanently separated from their birth families The Family History Book is vital. Not only is it significant in the promotion of genetic identity and the development of self esteem but also it is an important information source for searching and/or tracing genealogy, the placing agency and how to seek help and support later in life.

It is not disputed that creating Family History Books is work intensive and time consuming and it is for this reason that the child's Life Work Planning Group should consider carefully how this work will be allocated particularly in respect of information gathering. There is no reason why the work cannot be shared between a number of professionals and the child's current and past temporary carers. Corporate partnership, inter agency collaboration, working together, whatever term best describes joined up thinking is the way forward when considering how to produce a meaningful Family History Book.

However, it does need an identified person to co-ordinate this work and collate the finished product.

Sandra was married to Bill but he had been married twice before and had 6 children, one of whom was married to Sandra's uncle who was the brother of Bill's first wife and she was............

In recognition of the work involved in creating the books this guide devotes a complete chapter to Family History Books (Chapter 3, page 83).

A lot of work but for a child it could make the difference between traumatic survival and lifelong emotional security.

Now that's got to be worth it!

SECONDARY COMPONENT 1 -
Life Appreciation Days

Life Appreciation Days are for children moving on to permanent separation from their birth family. They serve a number of purposes and probably the most significant of which is a free flowing information exchange.

It is not unusual in disruption meetings, when a permanent placement has ended abruptly, for new information about the child to emerge and for the carers to say that if they had known that from the beginning things might have been different.

Life Appreciation Days can offer the child's prospective new family added insight into how the child responds to certain situations, what upsets them, what pleases them and what has been successful in responding to certain behaviours.

They should take place after the matching process and following the child's initial introductions to their new family. Whilst they are called 'days' they could be as short as one or two hours, this is dependant on the child's age and the number of people that can be mustered to attend.

The child's new family would be present throughout the meeting.

The day's facilitator will divide the child's life into relative intervals and ask people who have been part of that interval to come along and talk about their memories of the child. The best life appreciation sessions are when those invited people stay from beginning to end as one person's memories can trigger another's.

The guest list could include anyone from the child's old next door neighbour to their therapist. If appropriate, the birth family could attend. This is one meeting when the anecdotal can be told in abundance without anyone looking at their watch!

As they are designed to celebrate a child's uniqueness the information will err on the positive and therefore help build a child's esteem. The information from the meeting would be recorded and presented in two different forms—a factual recording for the new family and an age appropriate recording for the child. Photographs of the attendees should be taken, this is a great photo opportunity !

The meetings allow the child's new family to gain a lot more and different forms of information about the child than would be included in reports, and in light of the Essex ruling* this can only be advantageous for everyone.

The question as to whether children should be present at their Life Appreciation Day is a decision for the agency. It is advisable that children of an age and level of understanding should attend, however, this may not always be possible or appropriate.

* In 2003 Essex C.C. was successfully sued by an adoptive family for failing to give them full and pertinent information about a child they adopted whose behaviour later required specialist therapeutic intervention.

Photographs are an important aspect of Life Appreciation Days and would be included in the child's copy of the day (a digital camera would be invaluable in order for photos to be inserted next to appropriate text). Photos should be of the child's new family and each individual participant.

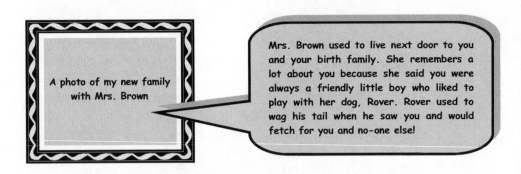

A photo of my new family with Mrs. Brown

Mrs. Brown used to live next door to you and your birth family. She remembers a lot about you because she said you were always a friendly little boy who liked to play with her dog, Rover. Rover used to wag his tail when he saw you and would fetch for you and no-one else!

The child's version of the day should be presented in a colourful, age appropriate and child interest appropriate binder. It should be clearly labelled on the front with the child's name, what it is, i.e My Life Appreciation Day, and the date it took place.

The new family's more factual version doesn't need to be presented so fancifully but it should look professional and laid out as one would present a conference report then contained in a Perspex folder.

SECONDARY COMPONENT 2 -
Later Life Letters

Later Life Letters are for children who are permanently separated from their birth family and adopted.

They are what they say they are—letters for the child to read later in life that give a more mature account of a professionals involvement with the child and their birth family. Of-course when a child reaches the age of 18 they can have access to their adoption records and therefore the factual account of the reasons for their separation from their birth family and the how and why the decision for adoption was made.

But Later Life Letters serve a different purpose. Firstly a child in adolescence but younger than 18 may want and be ready to have a more mature account of their past and whilst many new families are more than able to offer this, the young person may want confirmation. Secondly the letters are not intended to mirror adoption records or reports but are intended to state the professionals view and opinions of the child and their birth family and the decisions that were made.

The young person may reach a position whereby they want to talk to their previous social worker or other professionals involved in their earlier days and their birth family to ask their opinion, but those people may well have moved on and be difficult to find. In some cases, even if the professional was accessible, they may have forgotten certain details which have been eroded by time and a succession of other cases.

Later Life Letters are written at the time of the child's placement for adoption when memories are very fresh and vivid.

How to compose Later Life Letters...

An example of a Later Life Letter...

COMPOSING LATER LIFE LETTERS

The questions and answers...

How Long Should A Letter Be?

The length of a Later Life Letter is entirely the choice of the author, providing it has meaning for the child it can be as short as half a page and as long as a piece of string!

Who Should Write The Letter?

Any professional involved with the child or the child's birth family or the decision making process. There is no limit to the number of Later Life Letters made available to the child, in fact the more there are the more of a holistic view of the past is made available.

The obvious authors of Later Life Letters are the child's social workers, residential care workers, support workers and foster carers. But authors of Later Life Letters should not be confined to immediacy.

What about -

The reviewing officer, the child's social worker's line manager, and the adoption and fostering social worker.

Some may only write a page but it could be significant in terms of understanding for the child.

What Should I Write About?

By the time the child has reached the stage of curiosity about finer details they are probably well aware of the reasons for their separation from their birth family, what adoption means for them and have details about their birth parents and family history via Memory Books, Boxes, Photograph Albums and their Family History Book.

What they would be seeking at this stage would be opinion and personal memories. If you can think about the sort of things you would want to know if in the position of that child then this should form the content of your letter.

Where Do I Start?

The first stage would be to introduce yourself, your name, why and how long you knew the child and how you were involved in their life.

The next stage is to describe your involvement and not in the way you would compose a Court report but in the way you would talk about events and incidents to a contemporary.

Avoid any form of statements or opinions that lead to unanswered questions, for example if you were to write statements such as:-

"I found it difficult to work with your birth mother."

"I think she was frightened most of the time."

"Your birth father wasn't easy to get along with."

"The day I first became involved with you and your birth family was one of those days I'll never forget."

"Making the decision that you should be adopted wasn't easy."

"Your grandparents didn't want to get involved."

...and so on.

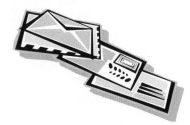

There is no doubt that anyone, seeking answers, and reading these sorts of statements would be left with the big question:

WHY?

Always qualify:

Why she was difficult to work with.

Why you thought she was frightened.

Why he wasn't easy to get along with.

Why that day was so memorable.

Why this decision wasn't easy.

Why they didn't want to get involved.

WHY?

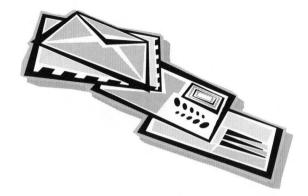

Much of the content of Later Life Letters may be based on opinion and not factual knowledge. In Later Life Letters it's OK to give an opinion providing it doesn't border on the outlandish, judgemental or a spurious value base but that it is based on sound professional experience and knowledge, and it is clearly stated that it is opinion.

The letter should err on the side of descriptive as opposed to factual representation. Set the scene e.g what was the weather like on the day you first met the child and how this impacted on your own feelings.

Later Life Letters should not be a chronology of events, it is not necessary to detail the whole of your involvement but only those significant moments such as the initial, the major life change and the ending, or just one of those, whatever would be more enlightening for the child.

Record your own memories of the child and your feelings for them. You could give accounts of the times you spent together and why. Tell the child about how they related or responded to you and what this meant to you.

Include your memories of how the child talked, behaved, what you did together and why.

How Do I Present The Letter?

In whatever form you feel comfortable with.

It can be set out as a formal letter in an envelope or be as creative as you want it to be, with illustrations, borders and artwork presented in a folder. It might be helpful if you include a photograph of yourself and/or places you spent time with the child, remember to clearly label the photos with dates.

Do I Develop Collaborative Closeness Or Maintain A Professional Distance?

As Later Life Letters are written in the here and now and are to be read in the future it would be impossible to develop any form of closeness or collaboration and therefore professionalism must prevail.

N.B Authors of letters should remain aware of their professional commitment, responsibilities and employment agreements to the agency they are contracted to at the time of writing the letter.

AN EXAMPLE OF A LATER LIFE LETTER

The example on the following pages has been written in the style of a story and it is highly unlikely that most social workers would have the time to write such a comprehensive letter. This is the optimum. As stated previously Later Life Letters can be whatever length you choose providing they contain relevant information for and meaning to the child. They could be just one paragraph detailing a particular memory you have of your involvement in the child's life.

AN EXAMPLE OF A LATER LIFE LETTER

(The names and circumstances in this letter are entirely fictitious and any resemblance to persons or situations is purely co-incidental)

1 February 2005

Dear Jean,

You probably won't remember me but I was your social worker for 3 years from when you were 2 years old until you were adopted at the age of 5.

The first time I heard about you and your family was when I was on duty for my team in February 2001. We all had to do a day of duty which is when we deal with all the calls from people who need some form of help or assistance. No-one really liked doing duty but it was a chance to catch up on the paperwork because you had to stay in the office. I remember very clearly the day I first heard about you because it was very cold and I had been late getting into work because there had been an air frost and I had to scrape the ice off my car. It had been fairly quiet on duty so I had been able to get a lot of my paperwork out of the way. Us social workers always had a lot of paperwork to do and I was always behind and never seemed to get it up to date.

It was just coming up to lunchtime and I had warmed up my soup and was about to drink it when the call came in. It was from a woman who wouldn't give me her name but she said she was a neighbour of you and your birth Mum. She said she had been worried for a long time about you because she had seen your birth Mum go out without you and not return for at least

2-3 hours. She knew there was only you and your birth Mum in the flat and was worried that you were left on your own. She said 'everyone' in the neighbourhood knew your birth Mum was on drugs and your flat was looking really dilapidated and dirty.

The caller went on to say that she didn't know your surname but knew your birth Mum's name was Gill . She said she never saw any people visit that could be family but there were lots of teenagers hanging around the front of the house in the evening. She said that sometimes there was music playing very loudly until the early hours of the morning and she recalled that there was at least one night when the police went to the house.

She gave me your address and hung up. I never ever found out who this woman was but she must have been a close neighbour to know all the things she told me. I'd say she was an older woman and she did seem very concerned and I didn't think she was just being nasty.

I knew the road you lived in then and knew it was council housing, it wasn't the best of areas, there were some decent houses but there were also blocks of 2 storey one bedroom flats that were originally designed for pensioners but they were now rented out to young people. I checked with the housing department to see who lived at the address the caller had given me. Housing told me the property was rented to a Gillian Pierce who was 20 years old and had a 2 year old child. I then checked our records for your birth Mum's name and there was one entry dating back to when she was 16. It said that your birth grandparents had asked for help because they felt they couldn't control their daughter (your birth Mum). From the records it looked as though someone had visited your birth grandparents but couldn't do much to help. I checked with the police and they confirmed they had been called to your address once because neighbours had complained about the noise.

I talked to my team manager about the call and it was agreed that I should visit but that I should take a colleague with me. My colleague Sandra Jones agreed to go with me. When we pulled up outside your flat it looked as if it was in a bit of a mess. There were black bin bags piled outside and some had been ripped open. There were dirty nappies everywhere alongside cans and bottles. We rang the bell and your birth Mum opened the door, she was still in her pyjamas, she looked thin and dishevelled. After we told her who we were we asked if we could come in , she was a bit reluctant at first but then decided to let us go inside.

Inside was even worse than the outside. Your birth Mum didn't have much furniture, there were no carpets on the floor and there was rubbish and clothes everywhere. Your birth Mum looked scared and cold, she coughed a lot and bit her nails. She asked us to sit down and started to move clothes and stuff off the chairs. It was cold inside the house and I was looking around for you but you weren't in the living room and I noticed there were no toys or anything that would lead you to believe there was a baby in the house other than the dirty nappies outside. I told her why we had called and asked if I could see her baby. She became very angry and used a lot of abusive language saying the nosey old neighbours had nothing better to do but spy on her. She was really, really angry and for a minute I thought she was going to hit me but she didn't and she soon became very tearful and cried saying no-one helped her and she had to do everything on her own.

I again asked to see her baby and, still sobbing, she opened the bedroom door. There you were dressed only in a vest which was dirty and wet where you had slobbered down it. You were standing up in a cot holding onto the top rail. There were no sheets on the cot mattress, which was filthy and wet, and the room was cold and dark, but despite this you stood there gurgling and smiling. There wasn't much in that room, your cot and a double bed with no sheets just a few blankets thrown over it. There were piles of rubbish, black bin bags and an ashtray full of cigarette ends.

I don't know who was more scared, me or your birth Mum. I knew I couldn't leave you there in that total mess but I needed your birth Mum to give me permission to take you. I began panicking inside about how I should handle the problem. Your birth Mum picked you up and held you so close to her it was like saying 'she's mine and don't you dare take her away'. You started to cry and your birth Mum looked around the room then finding a dummy she put it in your mouth, you stopped crying. The cold was getting worse, I felt a real chill and I was thinking I wish I hadn't come into work today.

Sandra and I managed to get your birth Mum back into the living room, she was still holding onto you really tight and you just sucked away at the dummy. It was obvious that you were hungry but there was no food in the house. I looked around for some nappies but couldn't find any. Your birth mum said she had no money to buy any. Sandra said she would go to the shops and get some nappies and food for you and your birth Mum just said 'thanks' without looking up.

Sandra nodded to me without your birth Mum seeing her, and I knew it was a signal to say "Shall I sort out a foster home?", so I nodded back.

When Sandra was gone I tried to talk to your birth Mum about how she was managing. She just kept crying or getting really angry. She said she had just been left to do everything herself and no-one cared and it was really hard. She said your birth dad had left her when she was 6 months pregnant and she hadn't seen him since then. She said she wouldn't ask her parents for help because they threw her out the house when she was 16. When I asked her about the gangs of teenagers hanging around the flat at night she told me they were her friends.

By the time Sandra returned with food and nappies for you your birth Mum had agreed that I should take you to a foster home to be looked after so she could try to sort out her life with our help. When you think about it she didn't have much choice really, if she had refused I would have asked my manager to get a Police Protection Order to enable us to remove you from your birth Mum's care. We never mentioned drugs and nor did your birth Mum, I did this on purpose, it would have been just too much for her to take in and besides the neighbour who had phoned didn't have any evidence of this just community gossip. But I wasn't surprised that people thought that way, your birth Mum looked like a drug user, thin, sallow complexion, shaking and often staring into middle space during our conversation.

It was getting dark when we took you from the flat. Your birth Mum had packed a bag of clothes for you but they were all too small or too dirty for you to wear. I'll never forget that image of your birth Mum standing at her front door crying and waving goodbye as we took you away.

I remember saying to myself—well this is where the work begins! You were a happy little thing despite looking very neglected. We took you to Mr and Mrs Williams who were very experienced foster carers. But all I could think of that night was your birth Mum in that cold and dingy flat.

Well I was right that certainly was where the work began. You will know the things that happened when you were being looked after because they will be in your memory book but I want to tell you about my involvement with your birth family. I started to get on really well with your birth Mum although there were times I got annoyed at her when she broke her promises or didn't turn up for appointments or contact.

She did have a real drug problem and was what we call a chaotic drug user. That came to light fairly soon after you and her went into the Mother and Baby Unit. She wasn't a bad person and she really loved you but the drugs had just taken over her life and that was all she could concentrate on. She had started on drugs just after you were born, small stuff at first, smoking pot but that brought her into contact with drug dealers who can be fairly persuasive in getting their customers onto the more lucrative hard drugs.

I met your maternal birth grandparents a few times, they found it really difficult to accept your birth Mum needed their help and I think they were really embarrassed by her being a drug user and having a child being looked after. They met you a few times and thought you were lovely but they said they couldn't take on your care because they felt they had gone past the stage of bringing up a baby and they were frightened that caring for you would mean having to accept your birth Mum back into their lives. They were nice people, quiet and a bit old fashioned, but had had enough of the problems with your birth Mum and wanted some peace and quiet.

When we eventually tracked down your birth Dad he was living with another woman. He said he was sorry your birth Mum's life had turned out the way it had but he had no feelings for her and their relationship had been difficult with lots of arguments and he had left her on a number of occasions before he eventually left for good. He told her he hadn't wanted children and felt that she had got pregnant with you to try to keep him with her. He said he didn't want to get involved and it was for this reason that he wouldn't see you. He said he didn't want to have his emotions 'all stirred up'. He was a very handsome man and seemed very self assured, he certainly knew what he wanted. When I saw him he was very smartly dressed, casual but smart. Although he didn't want to get involved in the care proceedings he did give me a lot of information about himself and his family for your family history book.

I remember thinking at the time how mean he was not wanting to be part of your life but then I thought—well at least he's honest and wasn't just going to string you along with false promises.

It was really hard trying to help your birth Mum sort out her life and it was like being on a roller coaster. She wanted to get back to normality because she wanted you back but she just didn't have the strength to carry it out. When she agreed to go into the de-tox unit I thought we had reached a turning point but that only lasted 4 weeks and she discharged herself. By then she had no place to live, she had given up her flat, and she went to live in a hostel. I used to visit her there quite often and she was always full of promises to do better next time.

There were times when her true personality did come through. She smiled easily and had a dry sense of humour but I think she was basically an unhappy person and was never sure what she really wanted out of life. I suppose in many ways she was quite complicated. She was bright but did some really silly things. Sometimes she would look sad and be all quiet and submissive. Then there were times when she would shout and scream abuse at me and I really thought she would be violent but she never was. I suppose a lot of her behaviour was down to her drug use but I wish I had had the opportunity to know the real Gill.

It was clear that your birth Mum was never going to turn her life around in time to care for you and you just couldn't wait around forever. That's why the decision was made for you to be adopted. It wasn't because your birth Mum was a drug user it was because of the lifestyle that her drug use created which could never include looking after a baby and helping you grow up safe and well. The department did try very hard to help her but nothing seemed to work, I suppose it wasn't the right time for her. But second and even third chances just kept failing.

The care proceedings were hard for her and that's why she eventually stopped coming to Court. She would never just relinquish you for adoption and once said to me that how would that look when you were old enough to understand, and so the Court dates just kept going on and on. There were times when your birth Mum would just disappear and no-one knew where she was living that's why it took so long for you to be adopted because papers couldn't be served on her.

I saw her once after you were adopted. She looked a bit better, she had put on a bit of weight, although she was still *very slim, and had met a man she was hoping to settle down with, he didn't know about you and she wasn't going to tell him. She said she was leaving the area, but wouldn't tell me where she was going and wanted to put the past behind her and that's why she didn't want to have any contact with you, she said it hurt too much. She said she felt really guilty about what had happened and was sorry she hadn't been able to change in time to keep you but knew you would have a good life with your adopters, she met them once and she liked them.*

I never saw her again after that but I often thought about her. She wrote to me about a month later saying she was happy and settled and was on a methadone programme to get her off the drugs, she asked about you. I've put a copy of that letter in with this one. There was no address on the letter so I couldn't write back to her and the postmark isn't very clear as you will see.

So that's about it really, it seems such a long time ago from that cold February day when I took the duty call.

I know I said I would never forget your birth Mum but you know I'll never forget you either, I still have a picture of you in my desk. I watched you grow in your foster home and I spent lots of time with you especially taking you to and from contact. We always sang songs, you liked 'The Wheels on the Bus' the best and I had to sing that one over and over again. Whenever I hear it now I can picture you clapping your hands and laughing.

You were such a special little toddler with a funny walk, you wobbled from side to side. When we arrived at the contact centre all the staff made a big fuss of you and there you were wobbling along and laughing. I used to give you malted milk biscuits on the way back to your foster home, you loved them, but I would get told off because you wouldn't eat your tea.

Whenever you had something new to wear you always pointed it out to me and you just loved having new shoes. You would spend ages touching them and saying 'noo soos', and you would tell anyone that spoke to you that you had 'noo soos'.

I was always proud to be your social worker I would take any opportunity to take you to the office to show my colleagues how wonderful you were and how you had grown. You used to like sitting in my chair whilst I swung it around. You would sit holding on tight to the arms and say 'swin' me, swin' me'. Sometimes we made such a racket that people would come from other offices to see what was going on and of-course they made a fuss of you and you loved the attention.

I don't know if you will remember any of these things but I know I will never forget them or you.

With all best wishes

Linda Smith

Later Life Letters can be as long or as short as you want them to be providing they are meaningful for the child.

There can be more than one Later Life Letter.

Think about the professionals who have been part of the child's life.

What about team managers or the reviewing officer or the person who supervised contact or the psychologist or the primary carer and so on...

If you were the child what would you want to know?

CHAPTER 3

CREATING FAMILY HISTORY BOOKS

When Birth Parents And Family Are Unknown

In the rare circumstance of a child having been abandoned, and subsequent investigations being unsuccessful in tracing their birth parents and family, the book should be renamed My History Book.

There are some aspects of the Family History Book which can be used in these circumstances such as the about me section minus family details. The History Book should begin with a full explanation of why there is no knowledge of the child's birth family.

There needs to be a great deal of information about where, how and who found the child, where they were taken and the events that followed. An age appropriate recording of the police investigation should be detailed.

The professionals and other people involved up to the child's adoption should be interviewed in the absence of family.

It would be worthwhile searching for any societies or associations around child abandonment so details of these can be included for future reference.

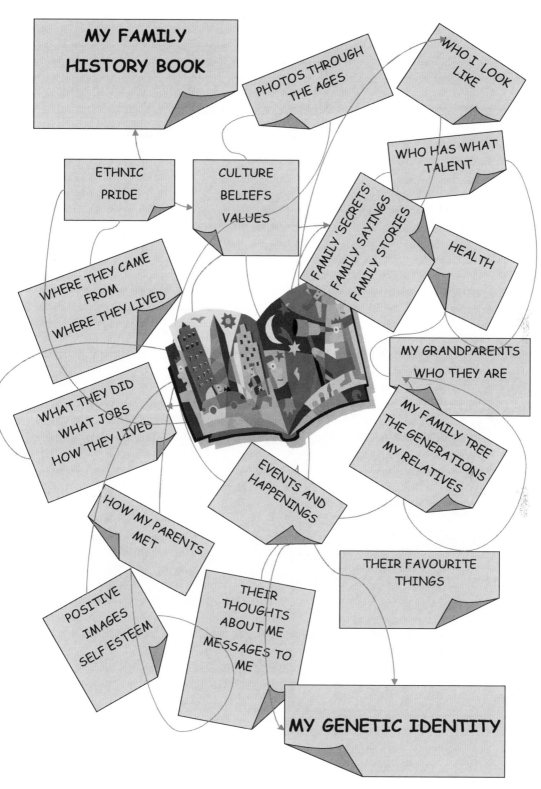

MY FAMILY HISTORY BOOK

PHOTOS THROUGH THE AGES

WHO I LOOK LIKE

ETHNIC PRIDE

CULTURE BELIEFS VALUES

WHO HAS WHAT TALENT

FAMILY 'SECRETS' FAMILY SAYINGS FAMILY STORIES

HEALTH

WHERE THEY CAME FROM WHERE THEY LIVED

MY GRANDPARENTS WHO THEY ARE

WHAT THEY DID WHAT JOBS HOW THEY LIVED

MY FAMILY TREE THE GENERATIONS MY RELATIVES

EVENTS AND HAPPENINGS

HOW MY PARENTS MET

THEIR FAVOURITE THINGS

POSITIVE IMAGES SELF ESTEEM

THEIR THOUGHTS ABOUT ME MESSAGES TO ME

MY GENETIC IDENTITY

CORE COMPONENT 4 -
Family History Books

Family History books are to provide the child, permanently separated from their birth family, with information about and knowledge of their birth family that would be freely available and accessible if they were living with them.

It is this component within the New Life Work Model that helps promote genetic identity, provide a positive image of the birth family therefore developing a child's self esteem. It should provide information that sets a base line for searching ancestry and genealogy later in life.

How Family History Books meet the life long needs of children is set out in the Introduction to this guide in Chapter 1 and does not need repetition here.

A HANDY HINT...

Family History Books require a great deal of information some of which can be started to be collated prior to final hearings (with the exception of interviewing family). As with a twin track plan, and when prognosis for reunification is poor, begin to consider what information will be needed and what can be gathered as proceedings progress.

FAMILY HISTORY BOOK

- Promoting genetic identity
- Providing positive images
- Building self esteem
- Giving information
- Offering explanation

If you are fortunate enough to get the full co-operation of the birth family and their wider family there will be a wealth of information to include in the book. It may seem that the book is rather weighty for the child but the temptation to exclude certain pieces of information should be resisted at all costs. Brevity should not be an aspect of the Family History Book.

A child's need for information will change at various stages of their life and whilst some information would be skimmed over at age 6 or 7 by the time they reach adolescence they may want a more in depth knowledge of their ancestry.

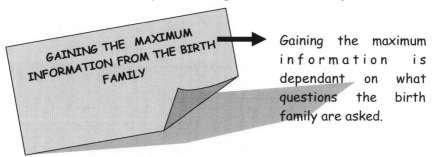

GAINING THE MAXIMUM INFORMATION FROM THE BIRTH FAMILY

Gaining the maximum information is dependant on what questions the birth family are asked.

As this chapter progresses through the structure of a Family History Book and what is needed, begin to make notes on the formulation of the questions you will need to ask to elicit the information required.

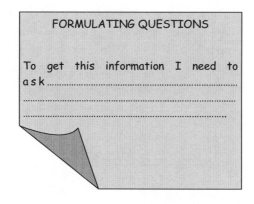

FORMULATING QUESTIONS

To get this information I need to ask..
....
....

Where To Begin

On first thought producing a Family History Book appears to be a daunting task but with careful planning and structure the task is simplified.

The starting point is examining what should underpin the production of any Family History Book.

* There can never be such a thing as too much information.

* All information is valid whether this is fact, rumour, or pure family fiction providing it is clear within the text which category the information falls into.

* The information the birth family provide will reflect their own culture and values. It is counter productive to the promotion of a child's genetic identity to impose one's own values and beliefs by sifting out what you believe to be good, bad or indifferent.

* In the case of information being age inappropriate reframing and explaining should be used, a more mature record of this sort of information can be given to the child's new family for the child to have an adult explanation later in life. The sort of information that requires this treatment is say if during the process the birth mother disclosed that she had been sexually abused as a child and this impacted on her functioning as an adult.

When interviewing the family you will need to clarify your duties and responsibilities in relation to child protection matters that are revealed during the process.

* The Family History Book is about the child's family and not about the child. For this reason any positive information about the family should be recorded which includes third party comments e.g from other professionals, previous foster carers, and social workers.

The recording of the child's looked after episode is documented in their Memory Books, Boxes and Photograph Albums and does not need to be included in their Family History Book, unless your agency has not been following the New Life Work Model and has not used Memory Books. In this case an additional section at the end of the book should document a child's looked after experience, or presented as a separate booklet, or complete a Memory Book in retrospect.

* No child, who is permanently separated from their birth family, should be denied a Family History Book. It is acknowledged that there will be birth families who refuse ,  are unable or it is inappropriate for them to co-operate. However there is probably sufficient information on file and within the agency and available information from other sources to create a book with some meaning.

The Starting Point

Identifying information sources is the starting point of a Family History Book.

Consider the who, how and where of information gathering. The most obvious source is the birth parents but they should not be perceived as the *only* source. Consider the wider family, grandparents, aunts, uncles, cousins. The wider family may well have additional information not known to the birth parents and they will certainly have a different perspective of the family history.

> In consideration of wider family consultation care should be taken that the rules of confidentiality are not breached and it is likely that accessing some sources of information may require permission from the birth parents.

Some suggestions for information sources -

- Family members, as many as possible

- Neighbours, babysitters, child minders, family friends

- Nurseries, schools, family centres, activity clubs

- Previous social workers/professionals of not only the child but of the wider family

- Case files, conference reports, review documents

- Midwife, health visitor

- The internet (for ethnic, cultural and origins/places information)

Gathering Information

There will always be some birth families whose pain and/or anger will prevent them from co-operating, perceiving this task as yet another institutional intrusion into their lives. This is more likely to be the case immediately following contentious care and adoption proceedings. It may also be the case that the birth family, given time to recover, will at some future date be prepared to participate.

It is important to explain to birth families the purpose of a Family History Book emphasising that it is for their child to have knowledge of their family and to promote a positive image of their genetic identity.

As many permanent separations include some link with the birth family, either through letterbox or direct contact, your agency will retain links with the birth family. In the cases of unwilling birth families following proceedings—use ongoing links to re-visit their co-operation in giving information.

Offering the birth parents a photo copy of the completed book will help allay their fears about content.

Putting this reassurance in writing will assist.

Some birth parents may object strongly to other family members being interviewed because the wider family may not be fully aware of the circumstances that led to the separation of the child.

Reassurance should be given that no discussion about the child's separation from the birth parents will take place and when interviewing this must be made clear to the interviewee at the beginning. It might be worth considering the need for written permission from the birth parents to approach their wider family and friends.

Once you have identified who should and can be interviewed it is time to decide how they will be interviewed.

- In their own home, at your place of work or at a neutral venue.

Giving interviewees the choice is probably the best course of action. You may have to interview some people more than once and this should be considered when setting up your first interview. Risks factors should also be a consideration around venue and in terms of being alone with someone.

- Record responses by long hand or tape recorder

You will need written permission from the interviewee for tape recordings.

The latter is probably preferable as nothing can be missed or misconstrued and it leads to an un-distracted interview. If tape recording is not possible it might be useful to have the support of a colleague to hand write responses. You should also make some notes in case the recording fails.

Tape recordings could be kept for the child to have when they are more mature.

- Face to face interviews or by questionnaire

Questionnaires are not always the best way to gather the sort of information needed for a Family History Book as they prevent sub questions which can lead to more in depth knowledge. However, if this is the only way information can be obtained from some family members then it is better than nothing. Keep the questionnaire simple—maybe just 2 or 3 leading questions.

Questionnaires are a good way of collecting positive comments about the family from other professionals/agencies.

As information is the keystone to a Family History Book then the gathering of it is the most significant aspect of its creation.

It may take some time but it should never be rushed or given a lower priority.

Remember—a Family History Book does not necessarily have to be totally completed at the point a child moves on to permanence although it should be in the process of creation.

Information gathering does not have to be nor should it be the responsibility of one person. Any number of people can gather any aspect of information and this should be a consideration for the child's Life Work Planning Group. The group should consider who is more likely to engage with whom, who would the birth family feel more comfortable with, etc. Ability to commit time to this stage should also be a factor in deciding the key players.

Obtaining Photographs

Photographs are an important part of a Family History Book particularly family photographs of different generations. They can be included on any page in addition to a specific section.

It is, therefore, important to obtain photographs during the information gathering stage. Persuading the family to part with photographs, even on a borrowing basis, can be difficult, especially those old and irreplaceable ones which could be the more significant. Making receipts for photographs borrowed and clearly stating when they will be returned might be helpful. By the same token you will need a signed receipt of return.

Photographs can be scanned, in fact it is far better to do so and the way in which photographs should be presented in the book will be dealt with later in this chapter under 'Presentation'.

Presentation

Presentation is another key attribute of a Family History Book. The book should be interesting and appealing to the child in order for them to want to read it or have it read to them.

It should be crammed with interesting clip art, shapes, and colours. Use lines of children's poetry (including the fun poetry), lines from songs or nursery rhymes or appropriate quotations to enhance the text, be creative! Using a pc and a good software programme makes the job so much easier. It might be worthwhile to make or have made a basic template for anyone in your organisation to use. The basic template can be re-coloured, have space for additional design to suit the child but with a laid out format of structure for ease of use.

But don't worry if this is not possible, it is the optimum, and a well thought out, carefully compiled Family History Book is just as acceptable providing the significant information is recorded.

I have seen a Family History Book that was handwritten in a plain page quality hard back book and it looked great!

The book looks better printed as landscape as opposed to portrait dimensions, it's just a bit more child friendly. Printing on both sides of the paper will help reduce the weightiness and use good quality paper, 130 -160g/m card is recommended although 100g/m paper is acceptable but nothing below this weight.

If you are using loose leaf then the pages should be wire or comb bound with a Perspex cover back and front. Or you could contain the pages in a good ring binder, colourful and matching the child's interests, **never** use any form of office stationery binder, they're too drab and dull.

When Family History Books are very fulsome you may find it better to present the family photographs section as a separate book. The books can then be presented in a colourful and personalised box for the child. Many stores sell good quality boxes at reasonable prices.

Photographs are best scanned and inserted. Pasting in photos can look unsightly, they can turn up at the edges, get damaged and worst still can fall out and get lost.

Whatever way you decide to present a Family History Book it should be the best it can be—

Remember - this is the child's heritage and it should be treated with the respect it so rightly deserves.

Setting The Level

*A*s the Family History Book belongs to the child it should be appropriate to the age of that child in its design and language. Consideration should be given to the child's known ability and stage of understanding and the level should reflect this. For children with limited ability and conceptualisation difficulties consultation with their new family as to what level to set the book at is essential as it is they who would have responsibility for helping the child make sense of it.

- Some information will need to be euphemised to ensure age appropriateness.

- Age appropriateness not only applies to the text but to any art work, design and poetry.

- Knowing the child will help, consult with ex-primary carers and the child's new family to find out the child's particular interests.

- Knowing the child will help you create a book that is interesting to them.

- If the new family feel it necessary, euphemised information can be separately and more maturely recorded for the child to have at an appropriate time in their life. (Some families feel they can deal with this without the additional written material).

- Keep it simple, clear and uncomplicated.

For children who are placed for permanency as babies and infants, and who are expected to attain usual levels of ability and understanding then the book is best pitched at age 4 - 5.

By this age they would more than likely have an understanding of their situation and the fact that they do not live with their family of birth.

Structuring The Book

There are no hard and fast rules about the length of the book, this will depend entirely on the information you have been able to obtain.

If there is no available information within a particular section then this should be clarified as to why, never omit a section. For example, if the identity of the birth father is unknown, for whatever reason, this should be explained. Failure to acknowledge the unavailability of information could lead the child to assume that information is being withheld. The consequences of this needs little explanation so it is far better to admit 'we just don't know' and 'why we don't know' than to ignore the fact completely.

This rule of not omitting any section applies to all topics but might have more significance for some children in the section about their birth parents relationship. Children born of rape, an anonymous one off sexual incident or an incestuous relationship need to have an explanation about events leading to their conception in the same way as any other children. Of-course, these situations require careful thought and sensitivity and will draw on your skills in communicating with children.

There is also the situation whereby the birth mother has relinquished the child because the child is the result of an affair. She knows who the father is but refuses to divulge this information. The child should be made aware of this fact.

NEVER OMIT A SECTION BECAUSE THERE IS NO INFORMATION AVAILABLE.

ALWAYS EXPLAIN WHY THERE IS NO INFORMATION.

The contents of each section of the book

The book is best presented as a 'dip in' book as opposed to a chronology or story type. Using sections makes it easier for the child to 'dip in' to specific information. The following is an example of how to section a book:

Section 1 -   **About Me** *(the child)...p.100*

Section 2 -   **About My Birth Mother***...p.106*

Section 3 -   **About My Birth Mother's Family***...p.112*

Section 4 -   **About My Birth Father***...p.121*

Section 5 -   **About My Birth Father's Family***...p.121*

Section 6 -   **About My Birth Parents as a Couple***...p.127*

Section 7 -   **About My Birth Brothers and Sisters***...p130*

Section 8 -   **About My Birth Family's `Ethnicity, Culture and Origins***...p.135*

Section 9 -   **My Birth Family Photographs***...p.136*

Section 10 -   **Messages from My Birth Family***...p.138*

Section 11 -   **Other Information***...p.140*

Section 12 -   **About Who Made This Book***...p.142*

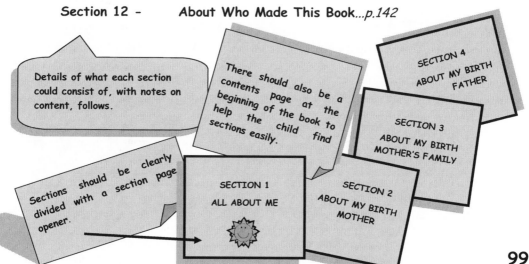

Details of what each section could consist of, with notes on content, follows.

There should also be a contents page at the beginning of the book to help the child find sections easily.

SECTION 4
ABOUT MY BIRTH FATHER

SECTION 3
ABOUT MY BIRTH MOTHER'S FAMILY

Sections should be clearly divided with a section page opener.

SECTION 1
ALL ABOUT ME

SECTION 2
ABOUT MY BIRTH MOTHER

SECTION 1 - ABOUT ME

*C*hildren who have a My Memory Book will already have most of the information in this section but there is no harm in repeating it. There may be additional information that can be gained from the family for this section which was not available for inclusion in the child's Memory Book.

As well as an additional information source this section is to develop a child's interest in the book (most everyone likes to read about themselves, children especially!)

Begin with the basics:

- Child's full name
- Day and date of birth
- Time of birth
- Birth weight and length
- Place of birth
- Where and when birth was registered
- Birth details
- Birth names in full
- Birth mother's full names
- Birth father's full names

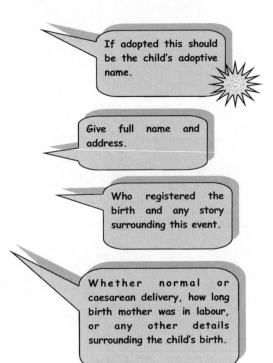

If adopted this should be the child's adoptive name.

Give full name and address.

Who registered the birth and any story surrounding this event.

Whether normal or caesarean delivery, how long birth mother was in labour, or any other details surrounding the child's birth.

If you are giving the birth family a copy of the book then the adoptive name should be deleted if not appropriate for them to know.

The next stage of Section 1 continues with more interesting information such as-

♦   **The meaning of the child's forenames** *(this should be all their forenames, birth and adoptive).*

♦   **The origins of the child's birth and adoptive surnames.**

If the family are unable to offer this information then the internet is an amazing font of knowledge. There are numerous sites that would be helpful.

You will find it easier to separate explanations about birth and adoptive names. If adopters have changed a child's given forename there needs to be an explanation as to why.

♦   **The reasons why the child was given their birth forenames and adoptive names.**

Who chose their names? Were other names considered and if so why were they discarded? Was the child called after anyone? Who and why?

Even if there was no particular reason for giving the child their name other than their parent or parents liked it, then this should be stated.

A 'remember' note - this is the sort of information a child would learn from asking or be told or just be aware of if they were brought up in their family of birth.

♦ Include events and happenings on the day the child was born.

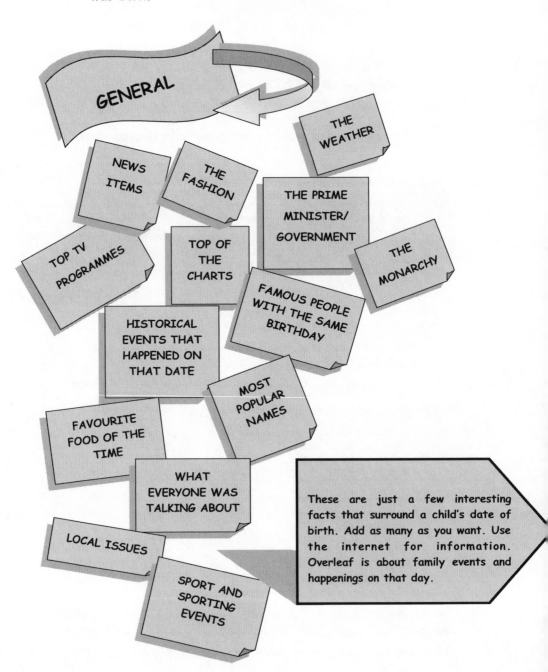

GENERAL

THE WEATHER

NEWS ITEMS

THE FASHION

THE PRIME MINISTER/ GOVERNMENT

TOP TV PROGRAMMES

TOP OF THE CHARTS

THE MONARCHY

FAMOUS PEOPLE WITH THE SAME BIRTHDAY

HISTORICAL EVENTS THAT HAPPENED ON THAT DATE

MOST POPULAR NAMES

FAVOURITE FOOD OF THE TIME

WHAT EVERYONE WAS TALKING ABOUT

These are just a few interesting facts that surround a child's date of birth. Add as many as you want. Use the internet for information. Overleaf is about family events and happenings on that day.

LOCAL ISSUES

SPORT AND SPORTING EVENTS

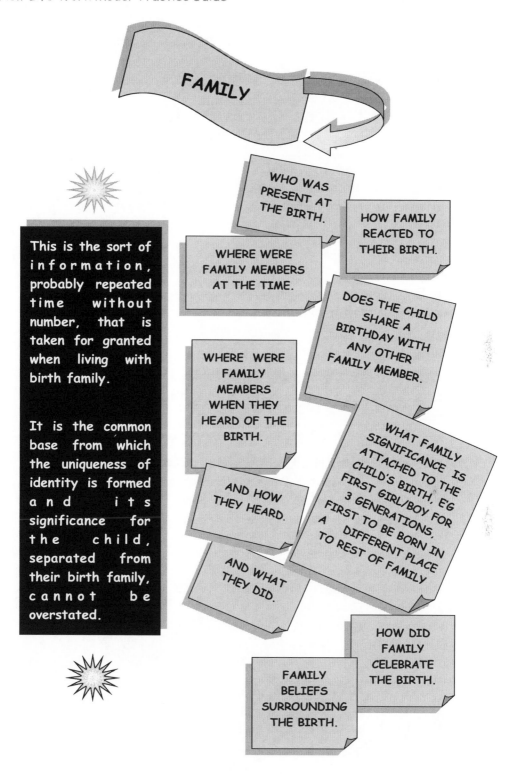

FAMILY

This is the sort of information, probably repeated time without number, that is taken for granted when living with birth family.

It is the common base from which the uniqueness of identity is formed and its significance for the child, separated from their birth family, cannot be overstated.

WHO WAS PRESENT AT THE BIRTH.

HOW FAMILY REACTED TO THEIR BIRTH.

WHERE WERE FAMILY MEMBERS AT THE TIME.

DOES THE CHILD SHARE A BIRTHDAY WITH ANY OTHER FAMILY MEMBER.

WHERE WERE FAMILY MEMBERS WHEN THEY HEARD OF THE BIRTH.

WHAT FAMILY SIGNIFICANCE IS ATTACHED TO THE CHILD'S BIRTH, EG FIRST GIRL/BOY FOR 3 GENERATIONS, FIRST TO BE BORN IN A DIFFERENT PLACE TO REST OF FAMILY

AND HOW THEY HEARD.

AND WHAT THEY DID.

HOW DID FAMILY CELEBRATE THE BIRTH.

FAMILY BELIEFS SURROUNDING THE BIRTH.

103

Ethnic, Cultural And Beliefs Issues In Respect Of The Child's Birth

Depending on the child's and their family's ethnicity, culture or beliefs there could be some significance attached to the day, month or year of the child's birth.

Their gender or position in the family may have cultural or religious significance. The choosing of their birth names may be linked to culture or beliefs, as would be a naming ceremony or admission to the family's religion.

These details need to be included with a full explanation of their historical importance and if the information is not forthcoming from the birth family then it's back to internet research!

The importance of this information, its relation to the child's heritage, and subsequent ancestral pride, cannot be overstated. This is one of those opportunities to build positive images of the child's family of birth.

A 'remember' note – this is the sort information a child would learn from asking or be told or just be aware of if they were brought up in their family of birth.

Using Additional Material To Enhance This Section

Stories about the birth parents' and the family's reaction to the knowledge that the child was expected always interests children. Whether the family thought they would be a girl or a boy, whether they arrived on time or were late, what they did in the first few hours of their life, how the knowledge of their birth was received, how people felt about it, what people did and said and so on.

It is extremely important to tell the child as many anecdotal stories surrounding their birth as possible.

Using children's poetry and rhymes helps enhance this section and makes it more fun and interesting for the child.

MONDAY'S CHILD

Monday's child is fair of face
Tuesday's child is full of grace
Wednesday's child is full of woe
Thursday's child has far to go
Friday's child is loving and giving
Saturday's child works hard for a living
And the child that is born on the Sabbath day is bonny and blithe, and happy and gay.

SECTION 2 -
ABOUT MY BIRTH MOTHER

S tart with the basic information -

- Full birth names

- Name now

- Other names she has had

- Ethnicity

- Day and date of birth

- Place of birth

- Address at time of birth

- Address now

- Places she has lived

- Schools/colleges

- Employment

> You will need to explain how, when and why there have been changes of names.

> Give as much detail as possible, such as dates of address change, what the home was i.e flat, house etc., and whether these places still exist, if they don't then explain why.
>
> Lists are good way of recording this information.

If a birth parent is deceased you will need to change some of the tenses and maybe delete some categories.

In these circumstances the birth parent's death should be dealt with separately from the basic information. The child will need to know when and why the parent died, how, who was with them, the date and the details of the funeral and where their remains are.

Details are important as too is sensitivity and age appropriate language, seek advice from a children's bereavement counsellor if you have doubts.

Check out how this has already been explained to the child.

Descriptive And Personal Information

Here some examples :

- Height
- Weight
- Build
- Shoe size

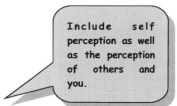

Photographs do not always give a true picture of height and build.

- Hair colour
- Eye colour
- Complexion

You will need to state if present colour is natural or enhanced and her true hair colour.

- Wears spectacles?
- Smoker
- Health matters

And why?

- Left or right handed
- Talents
- Interests
- Religious beliefs
- Political beliefs
- Personality

Include self perception as well as the perception of others and you.

My Birth Mother's Favourite Things And Dislikes

Here are some examples of categories:

If there is a story as to why something is a favourite thing or a dislike then this should be included.

My Birth Mother's Childhood

There needs to be as much information as possible, a mixture of the birth mother's own account and that of her wider family. Perhaps the easiest way of recording is as a chronological narrative with headings.

It should not be confined to facts but include thoughts, opinion and emotions.

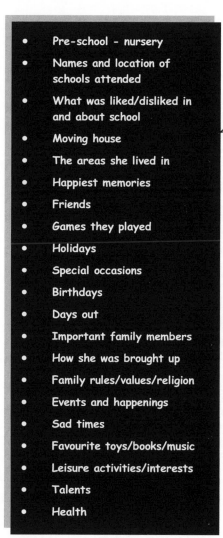

- Pre-school - nursery
- Names and location of schools attended
- What was liked/disliked in and about school
- Moving house
- The areas she lived in
- Happiest memories
- Friends
- Games they played
- Holidays
- Special occasions
- Birthdays
- Days out
- Important family members
- How she was brought up
- Family rules/values/religion
- Events and happenings
- Sad times
- Favourite toys/books/music
- Leisure activities/interests
- Talents
- Health

These are just some of the aspects of childhood that should be covered in this section.

Any special pet family names for her?

A 'remember' note - this is the sort of information a child would learn from asking or be told or just be aware of if they were brought up in their family of birth.

109

My Birth Mother's Teenage Years And Adulthood

Adolescent experiences set the foundations for adulthood and is often a time that is reflected upon later in life as to whether, with hindsight, the choices that were made during this period were right for the individual assessing them. It is for this reason that information produced in this section should be couched with the 'hindsight assessment'.

- Schools, colleges, qualifications, what was good, what was not, what could they have changed.

- Achievements.

- Employment - in more detail than previous section e.g exactly what their jobs entailed, which they liked best/worst and what they would have liked to have done.

- Relationships, if and how they altered with family and friends and why this happened.

- Other relationships, their significance to and impact on life choices.

- Friends, music and fashion.

- Interests, leisure activities—where they led and how they developed.

- Setting hopes for the future - were they realised and if not why not?

- Any involvement in criminality and how this began.

- Values, beliefs, religion.

- Development of political awareness.

- Membership of any groups, associations, clubs.

- Significant changes in their life..

- Health.

- Self perception.

My Birth Mother's Life Now

For those children who will have ongoing links with their birth mother, either directly or indirectly, it is still important to include this section as some of the information would not normally be appropriate to talk about via letterbox or during direct contact. This is particularly relevant to issues of feelings, hopes and aspirations.

Care should be taken as to how feelings and emotions are recorded. The child should not be led to believe that their birth mother's life is gloomy and morose. Nor should the child develop a sense of guilt about the separation.

When talking about plans for change it should not lead the child to believe those changes will result in reunification if this is not a possibility.

- Address now
- Who they live with
- Why they live there
- What they do, day to day
- Current interests
- Current friends
- Relationships outside of family
- Relationship with family
- Who they see and when
- Any positive life changes
- Hopes for the future
- Health
- Achievements

Achievements don't have to be sensational.

One example could be giving up smoking or making a new friend, they don't have to be great to be good.

Not everyone can run the New York marathon!

SECTION 3 -

ABOUT MY BIRTH MOTHER'S FAMILY

Begin with basic information such as names, dates of birth/death, where they live now etc. You will need to explain to the child the family members relationship to *them*, for example:

"This is your birth mother's father, he is your birth grandfather."

"This is your birth mother's niece, she is your birth cousin."

It might be worthwhile to begin this section with an age appropriate glossary to explain the terms you are likely to use such as, divorced, separated, married, partner, step family, half siblings, maiden names, birth names, family names, maternal, paternal etc.

Lists are a good starting point and then family trees, which are invaluable, so too are diagrams.

Include as much generational information as possible even if details get sketchier as time goes back, record the uncertainties as well as the known.

Try to get dates and places of marriages, deaths, divorces.

Include any information about religious ceremonies e.g baptism and where it took place.

Some examples...

YOUR BIRTH MOTHER'S GRANDMOTHER
(This is your birth great grandmother)

Birth name: Sarah Elizabeth SMITH

Born: 01 November 1919, Liverpool, Lancashire

Lived: In Liverpool 5 until 1960 then in Kirkby, Knowsley

Christened: December 1919, St. Anthony's church, Liverpool 5

Jobs: Line worker in Tate & Lyle factory, Liverpool
During the second world war she worked in Manchester in a munitions factory

Married: 16 April 1941 at St.Anthony's Roman Catholic church, Liverpool 5. to George Jones

Children: 8, 3 boys, 5 girls, 1 child died in infancy (Patricia age 2 in 1954)

Last address: 48 Roman Crescent, Kirkby

Died: 1 December 2001 in Royal Liverpool Hospital

Cause of death: Heart attack

Buried: Knowsley cemetery, Whiston, Prescot.

Once factual details as above have been dealt with then family memories should be added. If there is no photograph then a description should be recorded.

Any interesting stories about the family member, what their talents were, what is the strongest memory, any sayings they had, their temperament, personality, how others viewed them, their likes and dislikes, how they liked to live, what pleased them, what displeased them, their views on life and family. Who were their brothers and sisters, what position they held in their family.

Additional information such as early addresses and why they moved and so on.

Information about birth mother's immediate family could be recorded in the same way, her grandfather, her parents, her brothers and sisters.

Family Trees...

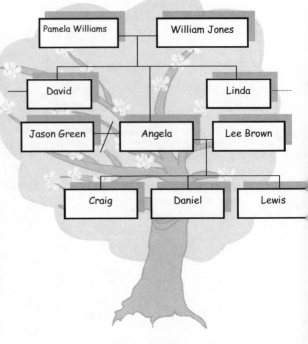

Family trees are a really good way of visualising family structures, however, they do need to carry some detail, dates of birth, marriages, deaths, full names etc.

If details are unavailable then approximates should be used such as year of birth, marriage or death. This can also apply to names when the family are uncertain about birth surnames but they *'think it might have been...'*

It might be easier to include a general family tree with the basic information such as names only then produce an additional diagram that is best known as 'BRANCHES OF THE TREE' that offers a great more detail and information.

AN EXAMPLE OF
BRANCHES OF THE TREE

Branches Of The Tree

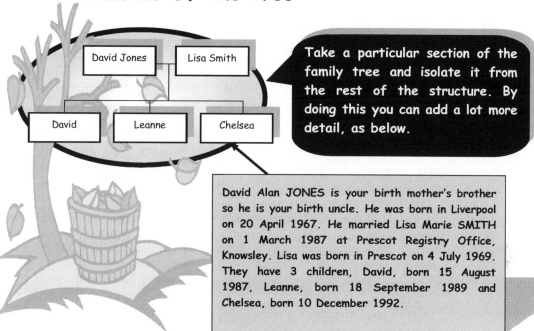

Take a particular section of the family tree and isolate it from the rest of the structure. By doing this you can add a lot more detail, as below.

David Alan JONES is your birth mother's brother so he is your birth uncle. He was born in Liverpool on 20 April 1967. He married Lisa Marie SMITH on 1 March 1987 at Prescot Registry Office, Knowsley. Lisa was born in Prescot on 4 July 1969. They have 3 children, David, born 15 August 1987, Leanne, born 18 September 1989 and Chelsea, born 10 December 1992.

David and Lisa have lived in Prescot since they were married. David used to work in the building trade but is now a taxi driver. Lisa works for Tesco as a checkout operator. David is White/British and Lisa is White/British/Irish.

Their son David is now at 6th form college studying for his A levels, he wants to be a primary school teacher. Leanne has just left school and is training to be a hair stylist. Chelsea is still at school and is very bright and in top sets for all her subjects.

They are a close family and enjoy going bowling and to the cinema together. The 2 Davids have dark brown hair, Lisa, Leanne and Chelsea have ginger hair. Leanne is very artistic, David likes sports and Chelsea is a whiz on the computer.

Family Tales And Stories

Family tales and stories are perhaps the more illuminating and interesting aspects of family history, no matter how outlandish or unbelievable, they all help to form our genetic identity. They are the common threads that help to bind family members together, a shared identity.

Stories about family members passed down the generations.

Claims to fame or even infamy.

Family 'secrets' which everyone knows about.

Family pride in something that has or had been achieved.

Links to historical events.

Family traditions and how and why they were created.

Pet family names and how they came into being.

The family scandals.

Family values.

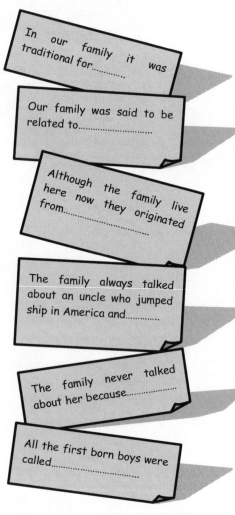

In our family it was traditional for...........

Our family was said to be related to...........................

Although the family live here now they originated from...........................

The family always talked about an uncle who jumped ship in America and............

The family never talked about her because.................

All the first born boys were called...........................

It is important for the child separated from their birth family to know about their ancestry and their shared genetic identity and how this was formulated.

No matter how incredulous the family tale or story is it must be included in this section. You could clarify which is perceived as a family fact and that which is a family rumour or supposition. Some of the information might be just one liners, it's still worth mentioning.

There can never be too much information!

My Birth Mother's Family Medical Stuff

Family medical history is extremely important to the child separated from their birth family as it has major implications for their future health and well being.

There maybe genetic medical conditions, disorders or a predisposition to certain illnesses that the wider family are aware of but this information was not available at the time of the child's permanence medical.

Questions about family health matters could be asked alongside social information questions or be dealt with in separation by ending an interview session with a medical checklist.

Whatever way you choose , it is important that every effort should be made to elicit health matters information.

Think of your own experiences of medical treatment and the sort of questions the medics have asked you.

Examples of the sort of information that is important...

A few examples...

- History of heart disease, angina, cancer, strokes, arthritis, diabetes, thyroid problems, high blood pressure, pulmonary disease, kidney problems, epilepsy, osteoporosis...

- Genetic syndromes...

- Genetic disorders, cystic fibrosis, muscular dystrophy, Huntingdon's chorea...

- Asthma, eczema...

- Psoriasis...

- Mental illness, depression, psychiatric disorders...

- Gynaecological matters, fertility problems...

- Deafness...

- Visual impairment, including who wore spectacles and why...

- Communication or co-ordination difficulties...

- Learning disabilities...

- Physical disabilities...

- Alzheimer's, dementia...

The list is endless...

On first sight, gathering medical information appears to be intrusive but this should not deter you from asking pertinent questions. Explaining the importance of family medical history for the child will help the already co-operative birth family feel less inhibited about disclosing these facts.

A great deal of medical information can be gained via supplementary questions about birth family members.

On page 113 of this guide we looked at presenting information about a birth family member. In order to gain the information you will have already 'hooked in' to this family member with the interviewee. A few supplementary health questions in this process are unlikely to be perceived as intrusive.

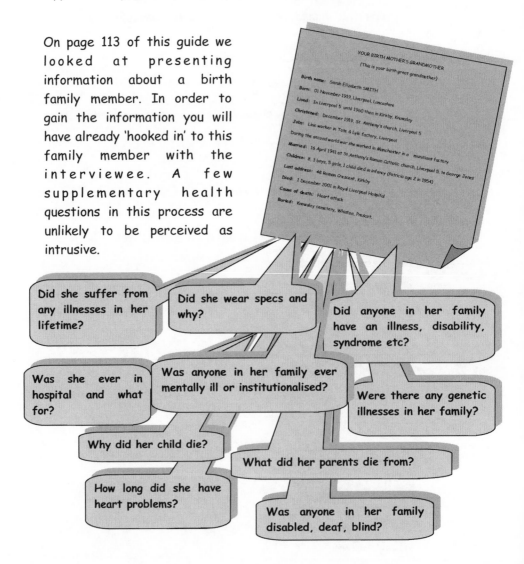

120

SECTION 4 -
ABOUT MY BIRTH FATHER

_____

and

SECTION 5 -
ABOUT MY BIRTH FATHER'S FAMILY

_____

These 2 sections should follow the same format as used to complete Sections 2 and 3 ('About My Birth Mother' and 'About My Birth Mother's Family').

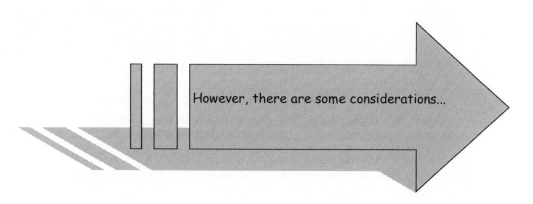

However, there are some considerations...

Dealing With The Issue Of Un-named Or Unknown Birth Fathers

This issue is likely to arise frequently and information and explanation as to why a birth father is un-named or unknown is extremely important. Failure to acknowledge this issue could the lead the child to make unreal assumptions or suspect information is being withheld.

Un-named Birth Fathers

In some cases other family members may offer their opinion as to the identity of the birth father but this sort of hearsay information cannot really be recorded without the permission of the birth mother. However, known facts freely given by the birth mother, which may not clearly identify the birth father but give some clues as to who he was etc., should be included.

> Your birth mother was unwilling to give the name of your birth father but said he was someone she worked with and had known for a long time. He was married with 2 sons and lived somewhere in Lancashire.

> He was a good friend of the family but your birth mother did not want anyone to know they had had a relationship.

> She didn't tell your birth father that she was pregnant because they had already separated when she found out, then she didn't want him to know about you because she didn't want him back in her life.

It will be helpful to the child to explain the dilemmas that birth mothers' are confronted with in some situations whereby the naming of the child's birth father could have serious consequences on their own or other people's lives. This is particularly poignant in care proceedings when agencies have a duty and responsibility to place children within birth families or seek the views of the absent birth parent.

It is likely that some explanations will demand another reference to the 'reasons why' used to explain deficiencies in parenting (see page 36 of this guide). A birth parent's inability to understand the lifelong consequences of denying a child their paternal genetic identity in favour of their own well being may be due to similar factors.

Whatever the reasons are for the birth mother refusing to name the child's birth father every effort should be made to persuade the birth mother to at least offer some description of him or what she knew about him.

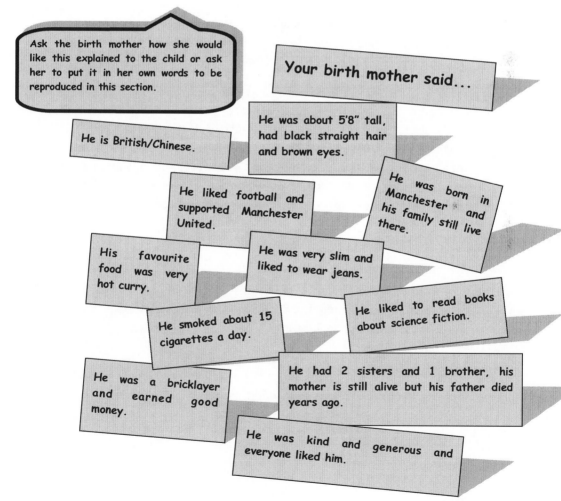

Ask the birth mother how she would like this explained to the child or ask her to put it in her own words to be reproduced in this section.

Your birth mother said...

He was about 5'8" tall, had black straight hair and brown eyes.

He is British/Chinese.

He was born in Manchester and his family still live there.

He liked football and supported Manchester United.

His favourite food was very hot curry.

He was very slim and liked to wear jeans.

He liked to read books about science fiction.

He smoked about 15 cigarettes a day.

He was a bricklayer and earned good money.

He had 2 sisters and 1 brother, his mother is still alive but his father died years ago.

He was kind and generous and everyone liked him.

Unknown Birth Fathers

Sensitivity is crucial when dealing with this particular issue.

If the birth father is unknown because the birth mother had a 'one off' sexual episode with him or she was having sexual relationships with a number of different men it can become a judgemental minefield.

If the birth father is unknown due to rape then according to the way in which this is explained it has the potential to adversely affect a child's self esteem, emotional stability and self belief.

It is worth remembering that information within a Family History Book must always be age appropriate, and explanation of these issues should reflect this. However, this should not be a 'get out clause' from explaining by just leaving it to the child's new family to give the more mature account later in life.

It is essential that the child's new family be given the optimum advice on how to offer an explanation according to the child's age and understanding and developing needs, and have ongoing access to support throughout this process.

Chapter 5 of this guide contains guidelines for adopters on talking to children about such 'adult matters' .

Explaining 'adult matters' to children is, in usual circumstances, an everyday event and the rules that underpin this aspect of explanation are just as relevant to children separated from their birth family as they are to any other child who asks-

"Mum, what's a condom?"

"Dad, what's a virgin?"

"Mum, what's a paedophile?"

"Dad, what does shag mean?"

"Mum, how do people get AIDS?"

Terms children hear everyday on the television, in the street or in school and the answers always use wonderfully creative -

All adults are grateful for euphemisms, they are the sort of 'mop your brow say phew' form of words that help you through those embarrassing, hand wringing moments when a child puts you on the spot. They also, amazingly, satisfy a child's curiosity with one fell swoop of a sentence.

Explaining adult matters to young children within their Family History Book relies heavily on the use of euphemisms that offer a baseline of explanation to the child that can be built upon as the child matures.

Dealing With The Reluctant Birth Father

Reluctant in the sense of not wanting to give any form of family background about either his or his wider family. This is particularly relevant to those birth fathers who are separated from the birth mother.

It is likely that in the case of birth mothers who refuse to co-operate there would be some documented information on file to give to the child. This is not necessarily always the case with isolated birth fathers. In these circumstances always record what you know even if it all seems a bit sketchy.

An example:

We know that your birth father had been married and divorced some years before he met your birth mother. He had 3 children by his first wife, we think they were 2 girls and 1 boy. The youngest of the children would be about 15 years older than you.

We don't know the children's names but they would have the same surname as your birth father. The family lived in the Dingle area of Liverpool and we think they still live there.

We think his wife's name was Kathy. We don't know why they got divorced.

SECTION 6 -
ABOUT MY BIRTH PARENTS AS A COUPLE

If the birth parents were never a couple this should be explained and you may choose a different heading for this section to deal with a one off sexual episode, an incestuous relationship or rape. You could choose a heading that a very young child is more likely to understand e.g 'How you were made'.

Children will need to know how they came to be in existence and whilst very young children are accepting of the fact they have only one parent, as they mature and begin to understand more about relationships they will question their own birth parents' relationship.

Being a couple doesn't necessarily mean having lived together, this should be explained. The child's parents may have lived in separate households but there was a form of a couple relationship in order to conceive the child. In the case of separate living arrangements an explanation as to why this was the case should be given e.g your birth father had another family and he lived with them.

Negative couple relationships need to be explained also, don't omit this section because this was the case. Explain that although they lived as a couple their relationship was not happy or good and say why e.g arguments, violence, fell out of love. The reasons why will need even further explanation such as your birth father drank a lot of alcohol and he would get angry, or your birth mother wasn't very good at housekeeping and they argued a lot because of this.

It is likely that even the most negative couple relationships began with positives and these should be highlighted.

How My Birth Parents Met

This will only apply to birth parents who had some form of couple relationship, whether positive or negative.

- Date they met, time, place and how.
- What they remember about that day—the weather, what they had been doing, how they came to be in the place they met.
- What were their thoughts about each other when they first met.
- How did their relationship develop.
- What did they like doing together.
- Where was their favourite place.
- How often did they see each other at first.
- Did they have any special names for each other.
- How did they treat each other.
- What are their strongest memories of those early days in their relationship.

The place they met may be well known to you but it won't to the child. Give a little background history, what was the place, where was it etc.

Did they like each other straight away, had they known each other previously and how did they feel about each other.

Is there a song or piece of music that reminds them of this time and if so why.

How did these names come about.

What were the big events of the time? What was in the news?

Are there any anecdotal stories, embarrassing moments, happiest time.

What would they want to relive if given the chance?

My Birth Parents' Life Together

Memories around this decision and the plans that were made.

What happened on the moving in day. If married, details are important, date, time place, who attended, why did they choose that sort of wedding, stories about the day etc.

List all addresses with dates. What kind of accommodation, why did they move, whose decision was it.

Who decided who did what? What did they enjoy about being together? What didn't they like about their relationship?

- How and when did they decide to live together/get married?
- When did they move in together/get married?
- Where did they get married?
- Where did they live?
- Who lived with them?
- How was their day to day life together?
- Who did what and why?
- What were their shared interests?
- What was good?
- What was bad?
- If their relationship ended, how and when?
- What would they have changed?

How did the relationship come to an end? What is their perception of the reasons for this? Their feelings about the end of the relationship. With hindsight, could it have been different, what would they have changed?

Are they still in contact? If so what form of relationship do they now have?

SECTION 7 -
ABOUT MY BIRTH BROTHERS
AND SISTERS

D iagrams will prove invaluable when explaining about siblings. You will need an explanation of the different terms.

If you intend to use the term sibling you will need to explain what this means.

Terms such as full sister/brother, half brother/sister, step brother/sister.

An example of this sort of diagram and explanation is illustrated overleaf...

A good starting point for this section is a short introduction about families and how there are many different sorts of family. Give some examples.

The above, of course, is for those circumstances when family dynamics are complex. Uncomplicated family dynamics would not require this form of explanation.

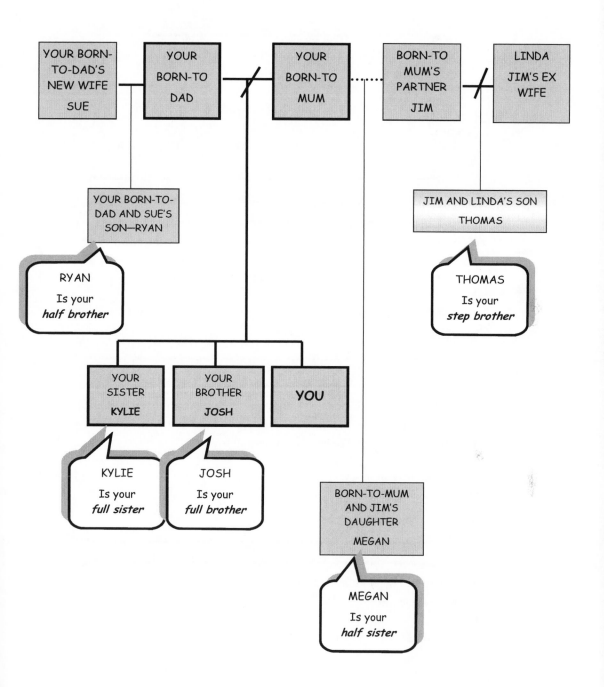

When born-to-mum and dad were married they made three children, that's Kylie, Josh and you.

Kylie is your **full** sister and Josh is your **full** brother.

Full means you have all got the same born-to-mum and dad.

When born-to-mum and dad stopped being married, born-to mum met Jim and they became partners and began living together.

Born-to-mum and Jim made Megan.

Megan is your **half** sister because you have the same born-to-mum but a different born-to-dad.

Before Jim met born-to-mum he had a wife named Linda. Jim and Linda made Thomas. When Jim came to live with born-to-mum he brought Thomas with him.

Thomas is your **step** brother because he is part of your family but has a different born-to-mum and dad than you.

When born-to-mum and dad stopped being married, born-to dad married Sue.

Sue and born-to-dad made Ryan.

Ryan is your **half** brother because you have the same born-to-dad but different born-to-mums.

Explaining half and full siblings through diagrams will also prove invaluable whereby a birth mother has had a number of children to different fathers.

In circumstances where a sibling remains with a birth parent when the child you are preparing the book for has been separated from them and adopted there will need to be a full explanation as to why this has happened.

Use the 3 part parenting model as detailed on page 32 of this guide to assist in the explanation.

Kylie, Josh and you were not able to live with your born-to-mum because she had troubles which made it really difficult for her to do all the things a parent needs to do to make sure you are safe and well and grow up happy and healthy.

Born-to-mum and dad had stopped being married and born-to-mum was on her own, and it was really hard for her to look after you all properly. You needed someone to do all the things a parent should do and that is why you were found a new family to take care of you.

After you all became part of a new family your born-to-mum met Jim and they made Megan. Megan is still with your born-to-mum because Jim looks after her. Jim does all the things a parent needs to do to keep Megan safe and well.

Jim will always need to take care of Megan because your born-to-mum is not able to learn how to do all the things a parent needs to do.

It may be helpful to dedicate a full page to each sibling, whether half, full or step and some basic details about each child:

DANIEL

Daniel is your half brother.

You have the same born-to-mum but different born-to-dads.

Date of birth: 12 October 1995

Born: Whiston Hospital, Knowsley

Full names: Daniel John Williams

Lives: With his foster carers, Josy and Dave Jones in Huyton

Born-to-dad: John Williams

Daniel loves football and playing on his Playstation. Daniel is not able to learn things quickly and needs extra help in school.

He thinks you are 'cute' and he has a photo of you on his bedroom wall.

> Even if siblings have ongoing contact details of them should still be included in the book.

> If there is no direct contact then detail the last time they saw each other and what happened.

> If siblings are separated it would be helpful to explain why this is and the differences in their status i.e living at home/permanent foster care/adoption.

SECTION 8 –
ABOUT MY BIRTH FAMILY'S
ETHNICITY, CULTURE AND ORIGINS

Whenever ethnic and cultural issues are mentioned there seems to be an immediate thrust of exclusive thought to minority groups. Everyone has ethnic and cultural roots and this section should pay attention to that fact.

Invariably, children separated from their birth families are placed for adoption or permanency outside of their birth family's community and, therefore, their birth family's culture. Even in the smallest of boroughs the cultural differences from one end to the other can be as different as spam and ham.

Whatever a child's ethnicity, birth family culture and origins this section should contain masses of interesting information. Maps, demography, history, beliefs, values, religion, poetry and general perceptions should play an important part in compiling this section and will take some research efforts.

In some cases the breadth of available information for the child demands a separate book and consideration should be given as to whether this is necessary.

SECTION 9 –
MY BIRTH FAMILY PHOTOGRAPHS

A s with the section on Ethnicity, Culture and Origins this section could be presented as a stand alone book.

Sam's
Family History Box

If presenting some sections as stand alone books it is better to contain them all in a box to go some way to prevent the individual books being separated and lost.

PHOTOS

ETHNICITY CULTURE ORIGINS

Photos should be scanned into the pages with explanatory text. If you have a lot of photos of different generations it is probably best to present them chronologically.

In presenting photographs there is yet another opportunity to give additional information than already given in the Family History Book e.g:

This is a photo of your birth great-grandparents (they were your born-to-mum's grand parents.). In the background is the house they lived in when they got married. They shared this house with two other families, the Waltons and the Simpsons. The house was in Edge lane, Liverpool and was demolished in the late 1960's to make way for a new access road to a new motorway, the M62.

Present photos creatively to make them more interesting.

Born-to-mum at age 9 months

Born-to-dad at age 2 years old

Born-to-dad on his first day at school when he was 5 years old

SECTION 10 -
MESSAGES FROM MY BIRTH FAMILY

Messages from the birth family could be helpful to the child as they mature because they are the actual words of the birth family and not just what you have recorded. By this the child will gain a further insight into their birth family's thought processes and the way in which they express themselves.

There is no doubt that some birth family members will want to and be tempted to write extremely emotive messages and your people skills will certainly come into play when dealing with this section. There will be a need to guide some birth family members on content with an explanation of why some messages will not be helpful to the child e.g *"One day I will come for you"*, or *"I can't wait until you are 18 and can come home to us, your family"* etc.

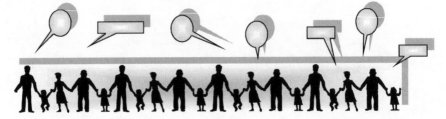

The messages do not have to be reams of pages. In fact it is better that they are brief and take the form of good wishes for the child's future. However, messages from the birth parents need to have a little more substance. There is no harm in the birth parents expressing their love for the child and their sadness at their separation but they need to be encouraged, in some way, to give permission for their child to be happy with, belong to and love their new family.

This is one section of the Family History Book that can contain 'paste ins'.

If the birth family are willing to write their own messages, with guidance of course, then that is so much better for the child. The child will have another insight into their birth family by seeing their handwriting and how they compose written work.

There will be some birth family members who will feel intimidated by having to write the message themselves and rather than omit it you should offer to type it in the book for them. If this is the case try to get the family member to sign the text.

It is very important to get the birth parents' signatures as knowing the birth parents' handwriting is yet another way of helping the child to connect with their genetic identity.

When brought up within your family of birth, parents' handwriting or signatures are something you could recognise instantly and, in fact, something you relate your own handwriting style to. Children separated from their birth family are usually denied this aspect of family knowledge.

SECTION 11 -
OTHER INFORMATION

This final section of the Family History Book deals with matters not specifically related to the birth family but to the adopted child or the child placed in permanent foster care and therefore permanently separated from their family of birth.

It is about giving the child additional information that is relevant to their status and possible future needs, and about the making of the book.

- Record the date the decision for permanency was made.

- Date of permanent placement/adoption placement.

- Date of adoption hearing, Court, judge.

- Name of adoption agency, placing agency and full contact details.

- State the law in relation to children having access to care files.

- State the law in relation to children having access to adoption records.

- Include anything relating to children's rights or the Human Rights Act.

- Record the duties and responsibilities of agencies in respect of support after adoption.

- List local and national agencies that offer services to the adopted child, say what their remit is and how to make contact.

- State how and when the child can request access to their care files and adoption records.

Researching Your Ancestry

Offer an explanation as to the meaning of ancestry. Explain that it is hoped there is sufficient information within the book for the child to research ancestry if and when they want to.

Explain that researching ancestry can begin by using some websites and list the ones you know such as ancestry.uk.

How record offices can help with released census findings, registrations of births, marriages and deaths.

Parish records are another source of searching.

SECTION 12
ABOUT WHO MADE THIS BOOK

And finally, tell the child who was involved in making their Family History Book. This information should be accompanied by scanned images of each individual and their part in compiling the book:

My name is ....

I interviewed...........................

My job is..............................

> There could be a number of different people who had contributed to the book and all should be included.

My name is ....

I took the photographs of.........

My job is.............................

My name is ....

I put all the information together

My job is.............................

> Apart from the above basic details contributors to the book may also want to add their feelings about their particular task and their memories of meeting the birth family. This information would be recorded in age appropriate terms.
>
> Contributors should write a Later Life Letter for the child to have a more mature view of their involvement with the birth family in composing this book.

CHAPTER 4

ASSISTING TEMPORARY PRIMARY CARERS

ASSISTING
PRIMARY CARERS
TO GIVE EXPLANATION

A Child Friendly Version Of The 3 Part parenting Model

*C*hildren need to have an explanation as to why they have been separated from their families of birth, but the explanation needs to be honest, meaningful and something a child can grasp.

Unravelling the complexities of parenting is a good starting point before moving on to the 'reasons why'. In Chapter 1 we looked at how Fahlberg's 3 part parenting model clarifies parenting, which was the adult version.

On the next few pages there is a child friendly version that primary carers can adapt and use in whatever method they feel appropriate to help the child's understanding. This version is designed for young children but can be adapted for any age, including adults. It's surprising just how many adults have never given a thought to what constitutes parenting—try it on family and friends!

THE PARENT THING

THE PARENT THING...

Being a parent is no easy job. There are lots of things a parent has to do to make sure their children are safe, happy and well. And they don't just have to do these things for a couple of days or weeks or months, they have to do them until their children are grown up enough to look after themselves.

There are 3 parts to being a parent and they are -

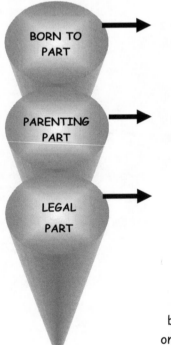

BORN TO PART

This is the part that makes us what we are.

PARENTING PART

This is the part that looks after us and makes sure we are safe and well.

LEGAL PART

This is the part that makes big decisions for us now and for the future.

All these parts make up the Parent Thing and parents have to be able to do all 3 of them all at once, and all of the time.

LET'S SEE WHAT'S IN EACH PART

147

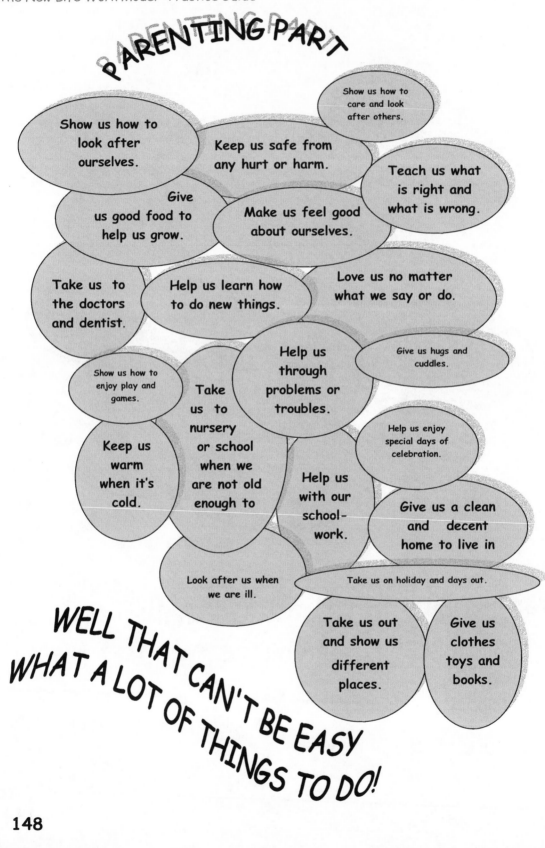

PARENTING PART

Show us how to care and look after others.

Show us how to look after ourselves.

Keep us safe from any hurt or harm.

Teach us what is right and what is wrong.

Give us good food to help us grow.

Make us feel good about ourselves.

Take us to the doctors and dentist.

Help us learn how to do new things.

Love us no matter what we say or do.

Help us through problems or troubles.

Give us hugs and cuddles.

Show us how to enjoy play and games.

Take us to nursery or school when we are not old enough to

Keep us warm when it's cold.

Help us with our school-work.

Help us enjoy special days of celebration.

Give us a clean and decent home to live in

Look after us when we are ill.

Take us on holiday and days out.

WELL THAT CAN'T BE EASY WHAT A LOT OF THINGS TO DO!

Take us out and show us different places.

Give us clothes toys and books.

LEGAL PART

Give permission for us to go on school, or other groups, trips and days out.

Decide what names we should have and make sure our birth is registered.

Give permission for us to join the army, or the navy, or the air-force before we are 18 years old.

Choose what religion they want us to follow.

Give us permission to stay overnight, or go on holiday, with friends and family.

Give permission for us to get married before we are 18 years old.

Decide what needles (inoculations) we should have when we are babies.

Give permission for us to have an operation or have certain medical treatment.

Choose our schools and make sure that we go every day.

Talk to our teachers and decide what is best for our future.

WHAT A LOT OF DECISIONS TO MAKE!

SO THAT'S THE PARENT THING...

So that's The Parent Thing - what a lot of things to do and think about!!

And another thing - parents don't do just one part at a time and then move on to the next part, they have to do all 3 all at once, a bit like juggling really.

Imagine how hard it would be to do all the things in The Parent Thing if you had troubles or problems or you were ill or your life was turned upside down, that would make it even harder, as if it isn't hard enough!

This explanation of parenting sets the foundation for the child's understanding of the difficulties some parents face.

When an explanation of the arduous task of parenting is coupled with the 'reasons why' some parents cannot achieve it, the child will begin to understand why they are separated from them. It will also help the child to understand that the separation is not of their making, nor is it necessarily that of their birth parents.

Playing 'The Parent Thing' Game

Using 'The Parent Thing' to explain the complexities of parenting can be visualised in a number of different forms.

It can be used as set out on the previous pages explaining each part of The Parent Thing and what it entails. Alternatively it could be explained in a more three dimensional way. For example:

Take four boxes making sure three of the boxes can fit into the remaining box. Label the large box as 'The Parent Thing' (or you could choose another name if you wish), then label the remaining boxes as 'Born-to Part', 'Parenting Part' and 'Legal Part'. You might need a secondary label for each box to explain the terms e.g.

'Born-to Part is the part of the parent thing that makes us, Parenting Part is the part that looks after us and keeps us safe, and Legal Part is the part about the laws (or rules) of the country we live in'.

On cards write out the various different tasks in each part of The Parent Thing, use one card for each task.

Put the cards in their appropriate box and put the three smaller boxes inside the large box labelled 'The Parent Thing'.

Make an opening in each box resembling a letter box opening.

When an opportune moment arises to explain to the child why they are separated from their birth family then tell them you are going to explain what parenting is all about first to help them (you may need to clarify parenting—Mums and Dads are parents).

Explain to the child that there are lots of things a parent has to do to make sure their children are safe, healthy and grow up happy and that there are three big parts to being a parent. Then open The Parent Thing box bringing out the three smaller boxes.

Open each of the smaller boxes one at a time looking at and reading the cards, also one at a time. As each card has been read and explained then post it back into the large box. When all the cards have been posted give the box a good shake explaining to the child that parents have to do all these things all at once and not just one at a time.

Then open the large box to look at all the things a parent has to do.

This exercise should be fun and presented in a play manner , involve the child, get them to pick out the cards, post them, shake up the box etc.

According to the child's age you may need to do this exercise in stages, if so start with the born-to and make this very, very, positive for them.

If the child tires or gets bored then abandon the exercise for another time.

Understanding the parenting part is the most significant aspect of the exercise.

The boxes way of explaining can be converted to suit individual preferences as it is important that whoever is doing this exercise with the child feels comfortable with it. It doesn't really matter how it is presented providing the following requirements are met.

- The exercise should assist a child's understanding of the complexities of parenting.

- It should be interesting and playful, perceived as a game.

- It should never be forced on a child.

- It can be repeated time without number, and is probably best done a couple of times at least.

- Whatever method is used to illustrate the points it should be child friendly and is best if it takes into account the child's current interests. (To begin with you could say it was about Sponge Bob Square Pants' parents, or Winnie the Pooh's or Mr.Incredible's, imagination is a key, before moving on to the child's own parents).

- When reading the parenting cards make some comments about each one, e.g wow, I know how hard that is, this bit's really hard, saying why and how you know etc.

- It shouldn't be a test for a child although there are ways in which you can 'test out' if the child has understood.

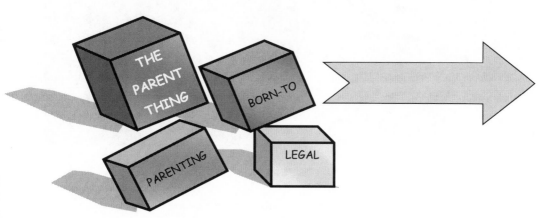

If the child has not grown tired of 'The Parent Thing' game you could do a reverse exercise to see if the child has understood it.

Using the boxes again, or whatever method you have chosen, take out all the cards and jumble them up, spread them out face up and ask the child to pick out a card. Read it, and explain it if necessary, then ask the child to post it in the box it belongs to.

Lots and lots of praise is needed when the child gets it right and if they get it wrong there should not be any form of remonstration, just skip over it or help them to cheat—again fun is the key word.

This reverse exercise serves two purposes, the first is a way of knowing what the child has understood and the second is that it helps reinforce initial understanding.

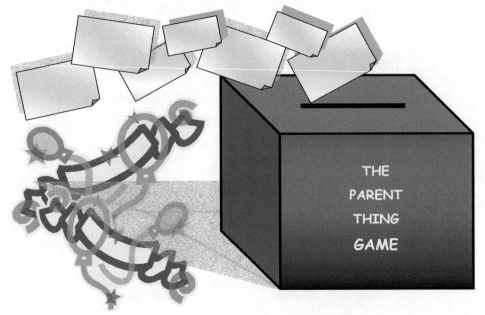

THE PARENT THING GAME

Explaining Why

Explaining parenting in isolation does not really give a child a full explanation as to why *they* are separated from their birth family. 'The Parent Thing' game lays the foundation for a full explanation as it is likely to raise the question for the child of why *their* parents could not satisfactorily complete the tasks of parenting.

Failure to answer this question could lead the child to believe it is they who are or were the cause of their parents' deficiencies. This is particularly relevant to children in foster care who witness, everyday, their foster carers' performing the parenting role with little difficulty.

Whilst playing 'The Parent Thing' game you will have already set the scene by emphasising how hard some parenting tasks are, especially if a parent has troubles or other difficulties.

It is now time to give a fuller explanation using the 'reasons why' as set out in Chapter 1 of this guide and repeated overleaf.

IT'S EASIER THAN YOU THINK...

The 'Reasons Why'

1. Their parents may have problems and troubles of their own that it makes it really difficult for them to care for others and do all the tasks of the parenting parent.

2. Their parents may never have been taught how to look after and care for others.

3. Their parents may be too ill to care for others.

4. Their parents may not be able to learn how to be a parenting parent.

5. Their parents may have been shown the wrong way to look after children.

What Goes Where?

There are no hard and fast rules about which circumstances belong in what category. In many cases the reasons why some parents are unable to parent may straddle more than one of the categories.

Set out below is a rough guide of what goes where. It is not a definitive list but it is unlikely that any 'reason why' does not 'fit' into at least one of the five umbrella categories.

> **1.   Their parents may have problems and troubles of their own that it makes it really difficult for them to care for others and do all the tasks of the parenting parent.**

Drug abuse, alcohol addiction, any form of substance abuse.. *Mental illness, depression, post traumatic stress disorder, post natal depression, personality disorders.* Debt, homelessness, housing problems, benefit problems. *Isolation, loneliness, no supportive networks.* Relationship difficulties, family difficulties. *Domestic violence.* Work related difficulties/stress. *Cultural, religious, familial difficulties/stress.* Unresolved issues from childhood, attachment disorder, parental deprivation. *Bereavement, grief, loss, separation.* Trauma as a result of rape, incest...

> **2.   Their parents may never have been taught how to look after and care for others.**

Brought up within a dysfunctional family. *Own parents having troubles or difficulties as in category one.* Brought up with domestic violence. *Own parental apathy.* Protracted institutionalisation.

3.   *Their parents may be too ill to care for others.*

Avoid at all costs using the 'ill' category as a cover all or a euphemism for something else. It confuses children and it will confuse you when the child starts asking when the birth parent will get better. If the reason is genuinely illness then an explanation as to the nature of that illness is needed and why a birth parent would not recover or get well enough in time to parent and care for the child.

Acute illness. *Chronic illness.* Genetic illness. *Terminal illness.* Physiological or psychotic illness including those due to self abuse. *Disability, physical and mental, including those due to trauma.* Degenerative disease.

4.   *Their parents may not be able to learn how to be a parenting parent.*

Learning disabilities or severe learning difficulties. *Mental illness, psychosis, personality disorders.* Psycopathy, paedophilia.

5.   *Their parents may have been shown the wrong way to look after children.*

Brought up within a dysfunctional family. *Brought up within an abusive family, sexual, physical and emotional.* Own parental apathy. *Brought up within a neglectful and rejecting environment.* Brought up within a violent and aggressive environment. *Brought up within a deviant cultural environment.*

THE LISTS ARE NOT DEFINITIVE JUST GUIDELINES OF WHAT GOES WHERE.

PREPARING TEMPORARY PRIMARY CARERS FOR LIFE CHANGES

An essential component of the New Life Work Model is preparing children *and* adults for life changes. For children their needs in this regard are identified and addressed within and by the Life Work Planning Group.

Historically the needs of the child's primary temporary carer have gone unnoticed and it has been a case of 'letting them get on with it'. Temporary primary carers have feelings too but their sense of grief and loss can manifest itself as them being unwilling to let go of the child or even building barricades to a successful introduction programme. There is no doubt that, not only for the carer's but also for the child's sake, these feelings need to be identified and addressed.

However, the temporary primary carer may find themselves somewhat lost. If they own up to their feelings would they be seen as weak or incapable? If they express doubt or concern about the plans for the child would they be seen as obstructive or possessive?

Temporary primary carers need to be given permission to express their feelings without fear of judgement or misconception.

159

The following pages form a booklet called 'Moving On...' to assist carers when the plans for permanency are defined.

It gives a clear message that the agency does understand the feelings of carers and wants them to express them without inhibition.   It also helps carers have a clearer understanding of the agency's expectations of them during the moving on process. Even the most experienced temporary carers have found that seeing the survival points, as set out within the booklet, in actual print has helped them. And for the less experienced carers it has helped them begin to develop their skills within a good practice framework.

Acknowledging the emotional roller coaster carers find themselves travelling on during this process helps carers normalise their feelings.

This is a crucial stage in the child's life in which temporary carers play a vital key role and therefore they need whatever assistance can be given to them.

MOVING ON...

A 5 point survival guide for temporary carers
moving children on to permanence

It's That Time Again!

The time you and many
other temporary carers dread, the time when you have to say
goodbye to the child or children you have cared for, helped
through trauma, worried over, had sleepless nights for, attended endless meetings about, fought their corner for, put
yourself out for and have exhausted yourself for.

There may well have been times when you had said to yourself,
"Why I am I doing this, am I mad?". And there may well
have been times you had wished for an end. But now the end is
here you can't believe the overwhelming sense of loss it brings
with it.

You are probably saying you just can't face or survive the
process of matching and introductions and more than likely
you are vowing never to do it again!

This booklet sets out to help you through the matching
process and the introduction stage. It is a 5 point survival
guide and its purpose is to help you move on as the child or
children do. Move on to enable you to do what you do best and
that is -

**Caring for children who are unable to live with their birth
families and preparing them for their futures.**

SURVIVAL POINT NUMBER 1

Letting Go...

As a programme of introduction begins and progresses you will find it helpful to consider, acknowledge and talk through the following with your social worker:

* How you are identifying and dealing with your feelings of loss and grief?

> LOSS AND GRIEF MANIFEST THEMSELVES IN MANY DIFFERENT WAYS, ARE YOU AWARE OF HOW THEY ARE AFFECTING YOU?

* How you are finding ways of coping with the child's/children's transfer of affections/attachments to someone else?

* How you are accepting the child's need for a different and new family?

* How you are coping with your own feelings about the child's new family?

> IT'S GOOD TO TALK ABOUT IT. YOUR SOCIAL WORKER WILL WANT TO LISTEN AND HELP YOU.

* How you are coping with the decisions about the child's future made by the agency?

* How you are coping with the extra responsibilities and work involved in an introduction programme?

> YOUR AGENCY WOULD WANT TO KNOW IF YOU ARE FINDING IT DIFFICULT AND TALK ABOUT HOW THEY CAN HELP YOU DURING THIS TIME.

SURVIVAL POINT NUMBER 2

Preparation...

Helping a child to prepare for the move to permanency is not just important for them but also for you. The preparation will help you come to terms with the loss of that child. The following could help:

> REMEMBER THE ANECDOTAL

*   Start a 'Moving On' book in addition to the child's Memory Book. Include photos of their new family, new home and new area they will live in. Include any significant stories and events attached to the introduction process.

> THIS NEEDS TO BE INTRODUCED SENSITIVELY

*   Set out a planner of agreed visits and other contacts. Let the child mark off each day and, if you know it, star the child's planned leaving date.

*   With the child's permission start packing their personal belongings and allow them to take some of them with them when they visit their new family. Agree with the child what they want to take or discard.

> TRY NOT TO SHOW YOUR DISAPPOINTMENT IF THE CHILD WANTS TO DISCARD SOMETHING THAT DIRECTLY LINKS THEM TO YOU OR YOUR FAMILY OR A SPECIAL MEMORY. IF YOU THINK THE CHILD MAY REGRET DISCARDING A PARTICULAR ITEM THEN KEEP IT SAFE FOR THEM.

SURVIVAL POINT NUMBER 3

Permission...

A child's ability to move on will be greatly influenced by your permission to do so. They need to know you approve.

* Explain your role in their life and how and why it is coming to an end.

> DON'T ASSUME THEY KNOW OR FULLY UNDERSTAND EVEN IF YOU HAVE EXPLAINED BEFORE.

* Talk positively and openly about the child's new family.

> THE CHILD WILL QUICKLY PICK UP SIGNALS OF DISAPPROVAL NO MATTER HOW SUBTLE.

* Talk about the plans for the child's future and new family as something you want for them.

> THEY NEED TO KNOW YOU APPROVE— REMEMBER THEY TRUST YOUR JUDGEMENT.

* Look forward to any visits or contacts with the child's new family.

* Allow the child's new family to continue their responsibilities to and nurturing of the child whilst in your home.

> REMEMBER APPROVAL—EVEN IF YOU DREAD THESE TIMES PRETEND YOU DON'T!!

> ALLOW THE CHILD TO SEEK PERMISSION FROM THEIR NEW FAMILY, IN PLACE OF YOU, TO HAVE OR DO THINGS. ALLOW THE CHILD TO BE AFFECTIONATE TO THEIR NEW FAMILY AND VICE VERSA. THIS HAPPENING IN YOUR HOME GIVES A VERY CLEAR SIGNAL THAT YOU APPROVE OF THE NEW FAMILY.

SURVIVAL POINT NUMBER 4

Encouragement...

The successful transfer of the child's attachments from you to their new family is vital to their lifelong emotional security. You play a key role in this process through encouragement.

BE PLEASED FOR THE CHILD THAT THEY ARE HAVING NEW AND DIFFERENT EXPERIENCES THAN YOU HAVE GIVEN THEM.

EVEN IF THIS IS A BIT OF A PAIN AND MORE WORK OR PUTS YOUR ROUTINE OUT.

NO MATTER HOW BLEAK YOUR FUTURE APPEARS TO YOU WITHOUT THIS CHILD.

* Encourage the child to talk freely about their new family and what they have done during visits.

* Encourage the child and their new family to make contact between visits via phone calls, texts, e-mail or letters.

* Encourage the child to move their belongings to their new family home.

* Encourage the child to perceive their new carers as their new family and, where appropriate, refer to them as the child's new Mum and/or Dad.

* Encourage the child to talk about the future and the positive changes it will bring to their life.

* Encourage the child to identify with their new family.

ALTHOUGH IT HURTS TO HEAR THE CHILD TALK ABOUT THE WAY THEIR NEW FAMILY DOES OR DOESN'T DO THINGS WHICH IS SOMEWHAT ALIEN TO YOURSELF ALLOW THEM TO CHANGE AND VALUE THEIR NEW FAMILY'S WAY OF LIFE.

SURVIVAL POINT NUMBER 5

Being Positive...

Being positive may be the most difficult task of all and yet it is probably one of the most important.

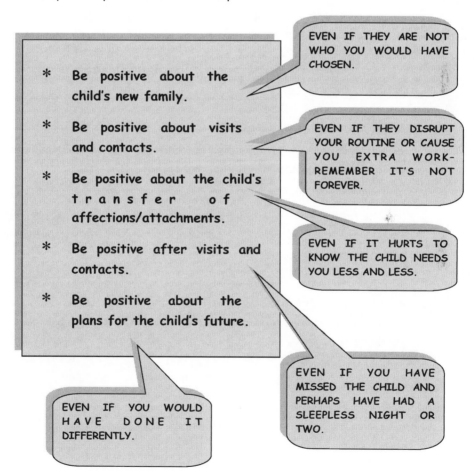

* Be positive about the child's new family.

EVEN IF THEY ARE NOT WHO YOU WOULD HAVE CHOSEN.

* Be positive about visits and contacts.

EVEN IF THEY DISRUPT YOUR ROUTINE OR CAUSE YOU EXTRA WORK- REMEMBER IT'S NOT FOREVER.

* Be positive about the child's transfer of affections/attachments.

EVEN IF IT HURTS TO KNOW THE CHILD NEEDS YOU LESS AND LESS.

* Be positive after visits and contacts.

* Be positive about the plans for the child's future.

EVEN IF YOU WOULD HAVE DONE IT DIFFERENTLY.

EVEN IF YOU HAVE MISSED THE CHILD AND PERHAPS HAVE HAD A SLEEPLESS NIGHT OR TWO.

A FINAL THOUGHT

"There is always one
moment in childhood
When the door opens
and lets the future in."

The Power and the Glory,
Graham Greene, 1940

The role you play in helping a child move on to permanence and their future is not just important—it is vital.

For the child the journey to their future begins when the decision for permanency is made and not when they move into their new family's home.

You are the principal guide in the first part of this journey because at this stage you are the person the child trusts the most. Travelling positively with them and making it an enjoyable experience will help them be well prepared for their new life and the years of future that lay before them.

Being positive about the introduction process will also help you survive this difficult time and enable you to move on and begin again to help other children prepare for their futures.

CHAPTER 5

ASSISTING ADOPTERS IN THE TELLING PROCESS

THE TELLING PROCESS

Telling is a process, it's not a one off task that once done never needs revisiting. Giving information and explanation to children changes as they grow and mature and demand more detailed answers to their ever probing questions.

when?

who?

why?

Adopters need a starting point, a baseline, a platform from which to begin.

The following pages take the form of guidelines for adoptive parents.

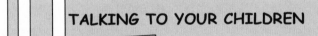

TALKING TO YOUR CHILDREN

This booklet can be converted to a presentation and used in an adoption support group. It provokes a good debate and discussion.

TALKING TO YOUR CHILDREN

Guidelines to assist adopters in the 'telling process'

The Telling Process

The telling process isn't just about telling a child they are adopted, it's about giving them information and explanation. It's called a process because it never is a one off task, it changes and evolves as a child grows into maturity.

The first stage of the process is about telling your child they are adopted. Easy, some might say—but not so. This first step is just as difficult as explaining to a child **why** they were separated from their birth family in the first place.

We have all seen the documentaries, read the books, the newspaper articles about adults who learned later in life that they were adopted and how this impacted on their life. We have all heard the sharp intakes of breath, the 'tut-tuts' at adopters who appeared to 'fail' in their parental responsibility of informing and explaining. But seldom do we hear about the difficulties adopters face within the telling process.

In today's adoptive world, not telling probably owes more to fear of consequence as opposed to conscious concealment.

LET'S SEE WHAT SOME ADOPTERS SAID ABOUT THE TELLING PROCESS...

From a single adoptive mother whose child was placed with her when he was 2 years old and adopted 6 months later...

"I promised myself I would tell him he was adopted the minute he was able to converse. I was all keyed up to do so, but then, opportunities just seemed to pass me by. I think I was scared, I certainly didn't feel confident about it.

I found myself telling lies and I felt really guilty and frightened that he would find out from someone else, but I really didn't know where to begin.

I was getting really anxious about it then one day, when he was 7, I just blurted it out over the dinner table. He was a bit puzzled at first but once I had said it I felt more confident about explaining what it meant.

It seemed like an eternity before he said anything and then all he said was "Can I go out and play now, Mum?"

We talk about it a lot now. I wish I had done it earlier and saved myself all those anxieties."

The telling is not just difficult for adoptive parents, it impacts on future generations.

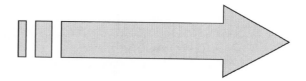

When adopters become grandparents...

"Our daughter was 9 when she was placed for adoption with us. One of the many advantages of adopting an older child is that you don't have to tie yourself up in knots about the telling bit, they know it already. In our house adoption was an open topic and it felt fine and comfortable. It was from this comfortable position that we were critical of adopters who didn't tell their children they were adopted at an early age.

It was only when our daughter had her first child, our first grandchild, that we realised just how difficult the telling is. We were really troubled and asked ourselves the question 'How do we tell this adorable child, who was very much our own, that he had no genetic links to us whatsoever?' Even our daughter wasn't sure she wanted him to know she was adopted.

He was 5 when he was told, with grateful thanks to the film 'Pollyanna' which opened a door of opportunity.

He is now 13 and the lack of genetic links has made absolutely no difference to the way he loves us and we love him. In fact in some strange way I think it has given a greater strength to our relationship with him."

The telling is not just about informing about adoption it's also about giving explanations.

HAVING TO EXPLAIN...

From adopters who had to explain rejection...

"Our son was 6 when he came to live with us. He'd had a pretty rough time. His birth mother was a chaotic drug user and her lifestyle couldn't include caring for a 3 year old. He'd witnessed all sorts of things children just shouldn't know about. She agreed to him being looked after and social services approved his grandparents as his foster carers.

He only lived with them for a few months before they asked for him to be removed because they couldn't cope with his behaviour. He was placed with temporary foster carers. They really helped him and he grew very attached to them, well he was there for over 2 years.

When we met him he knew all about adoption and what it would mean for him. He settled into our family very quickly, but then, after he was adopted, he started to 'play up' really quite badly. He'd get in a real tantrum about the most trivial of things, he'd scream and shout and cry and was forever saying that no-one loved him and no-one wanted him.

It was clear to us that whilst he had been told about adoption no-one had ever explained to him why his birth mother and grandparents had acted the way they did. Nor had anyone explained why his foster carers hadn't adopted him themselves.

We knew we would have to explain this to him and that it would be really difficult, talk about sleepless nights! Just when and how do you explain those things to a little boy who was obviously hurting deeply? We knew we needed help but felt a bit embarrassed about asking the adoption agency, we thought they would think we were useless or something like that. We did it anyway and they were really helpful.

He's having play therapy now and we are being tutored in filial play therapy so we can continue it at home. It feels good that we are doing something for him and the support is invaluable."

The telling really is a lifelong process with many different facets, this is the reality of what adopters have to face—so no easy task, but with help it can be easier.

175

THE IMPORTANCE OF THE TELLING PROCESS

There are very sound reasons for the telling process not only in terms of your child's lifelong emotional security but also in relation to your lifelong relationship with them, and it isn't only about explaining adoption.

♦ Every child has the right to information about themselves and their family of origin.

> Imagine what it must feel like to discover that family, friends and even neighbours knew something very personal about you that you didn't know about yourself because your parents hadn't told you.

> Imagine how you would feel if you discovered your parents hadn't told you something very important about yourself.

> Imagine the trauma to your child if someone other than you inadvertently told them they were adopted.

♦ When your child reaches the age of 18 they can have access to their care files and adoption records. It could be extremely traumatic for them to discover that you have withheld information from them.

> Your child will know that whatever is in their care files and adoption records would have been made known to you. Imagine their feelings at knowing the questions they had asked you about certain information had gone unanswered because you said you didn't know.

- Information about their origins is a key component in building your child's genetic identity and emotional security.

"It is difficult to grow up as a psychologically healthy adult if denied access to one's own history."

A Child's Journey through Placement

Vera Fahlberg, BAAF 1994

- Information offers explanation.

- Explanation gives your child permission to grieve for the loss of their birth family. The process will assist your child's healthy emotional growth. Without this process a child's emotional development could be impaired.

"When a person is unable to complete a mourning task from childhood, he either has to surrender his emotions in order that they do not suddenly overwhelm him or else he may be haunted constantly throughout his life with sadness for which he can never find an appropriate explanation."

Loss and Grief, Schoenberg et al. 1970

Children grieve for the loss of their origins and ancestry even when they have been adopted in infancy and have no recollection of their birth family.

177

From the David Brodzinsky et al. book (1993)
"Being Adopted: The Lifelong Search for Self"

"Sarah was a perfectly happy, well-adjusted seventeen year old, who was adopted as an infant. She always knew she was adopted, and always felt comfortable and loved in her adoptive family. Nonetheless, Sarah had a vague sense of longing:

'Sometimes I feel incomplete, Sarah told us. I need to know more. Why did it happen? What is she like? Who is my birth father? What is he like? The older I get the more important it is to know. It's pretty frustrating being an adoptee sometimes."

For children who have been separated from their birth families, at no matter what age, there could always be a sense of being incomplete, because out there somewhere is their history, their genetic identity, their ancestry.

It isn't just about telling them they are adopted and what that means, although very important in itself, it's about giving them information and explanation why, what happened, who their birth family are and what they are like.

Where To Begin?

It seems like a mammoth task, so much information and explanation that it's difficult to know when and how to feed it to your child. But there is an old adage that might help:

Question:

How do you eat an elephant?

Answer:

In small chunks!

Begin with some basic preparations...

Addressing Your Own Fears
And Concerns

Fear about the consequences of telling is probably the most common underlying reason for avoiding the issue. Think about what it is that frightens you about this process.

♦   **Identify your own fears about telling.**

What are they? Where do they come from? Why do they exist?

♦   **Rationalise your fears.**

What are they based on? Are they based on reality or your worst nightmares?

♦   **Deal with your fears.**

How can you overcome them? Who can help ? What help do you need?

Be Prepared To Be Honest

*"O, what a tangled web we weave,
When first we practice to deceive!"*

Sir Walter Scott, 1808

No-one sets out to consciously deceive their child but deception is how your child could perceive it later in life. Beginning with honesty and continuing it throughout the process will help even if at times it demands a little more thought and effort. It is true to say that...

♦ One untruth easily leads to many more. It is by far more difficult to undo a tangle of deceit than it is to actually start with honesty.

♦ If dishonesty in the 'telling' is discovered by your child, at whatever age, trust can be destroyed or seriously shaken. Any other information you have given your child, no matter how truthful, could be questioned.

Prepare Yourself For 'Telling'

Y ou don't have to go into rigorous training to prepare yourself for telling, simply make some basic preparations.

♦ Think about the information you have and how you will convert this into age appropriate terms for your child to understand.

♦ If you think the information is lacking then contact your adoption agency and ask for help.

♦ You know your child better than anyone. Think about the way in which to best present the information, how they are likely to respond, what questions they are likely to ask and how you will answer them.

Using Opportunity

There are no rules about time or place. If an opportunity arises, no matter what you are doing or where you are, then grab it, seize it, take it, use it!

♦ Telling doesn't need to be formal in fact it's far better that it is not. It should be relaxed and comfortable.

♦ It doesn't have to be all at once. Lay foundations, feed information slowly. Nor does it have to be chronological, you don't have to start at the beginning and end at the end. It all depends on what opportunities arise for what piece of information.

♦ Use everyday events and happenings to explain. There will always be opportunities whilst watching television, a film, reading a story, or a family event you can relate information to.

Have Confidence In Yourself

Having confidence in your ability to answer your child's questions will make the task much easier, you will feel relaxed and so too will your child. Thus giving them the confidence to talk freely about any issue relating to their separation from their birth family and adoption. When they feel uninhibited they will ask questions resulting in your task of giving information and explanation so much easier.

♦   You have the skills—it is highly unlikely you would have been approved as an adopter if there was a shortfall in, or a lack of potential to develop, the skills required to undertake the 'telling process'.

♦   Don't be afraid to admit to your child about not knowing something. No-one has all the answers all of the time.

♦   If something is difficult to explain—own up to it and tell your child you need to think about it or get more information before answering a certain question.

Listening

In the telling process listening to what your child is asking you is just as important as what you are telling your child.

A story...

> A young child once asked his father –
>
> "Dad, where do I come from?"
>
> His father realised that the time he had been dreading had arrived. The time he would have to explain to his child the facts of life.
>
> The father sat his child down, looked earnestly into the child's face and with a sense of acute embarrassment told his son, in great detail, the facts of life.
>
> The child listened intently and when he was sure his father had finished he looked at him seriously and said:
>
> "Thanks for telling me that, Dad, but where do I come from?
>
> Do I come from the North West, the South East, the North East...

And the moral of the story is...

◆ Be sure you know what your child is asking and you understand the meaning of their questions.

◆ Double check their questions before answering.

Giving Reassurance

---

*C*hildren separated from their families of birth can often 'blame' themselves for the separation. In the explanation stage it is important to give reassurance that there is no blame attached to *anyone*. Their separation is due to a set or sets of circumstances.

♦   Reassure your child that they are not responsible for the actions of their birth family, there are reasons and explanations for everything.

> **Reasons why are detailed later in this booklet.**

♦   Reassure your child that the actions and behaviour of their birth family, either pre or post separation, are not inherited.

> **Some behaviours could be the result of illness which the birth family may have a genetic pre-disposition for, and this should be dealt with separately after gaining as much knowledge as possible about the condition. Actions and behaviours talked about here are those which have no physiological or psychotic base.**

♦   Reassure your child that whatever the actions or behaviour of their birth family it does not affect the love you have for them.

> **The actions and behaviours may be socially or morally unacceptable or criminal. Your child needs to know that you do not perceive *them* as unacceptable because of their genetic links.**

Explaining Adoption And What It Means

It is not enough to tell your child they are adopted, they need to understand exactly what that term means. To a child the legal complexities of adoption can be very confusing and explanation needs to suit their age and understanding. But before offering some guidelines on how this can be achieved there are some points to consider.

Firstly we have to reconsider the issue of honesty:

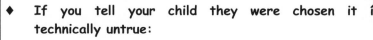

♦ **If you tell your child they were chosen it is technically untrue:**

*In truth it was **you** who was chosen for your child.*

♦ **If you tell your child they are special because they are adopted:**

Is being abused, ill treated, neglected or rejected special? They may be special to you because they are the child you wanted and needed so much, clarify and differentiate.

♦ **If you explain adoption but not why you needed to adopt:**

Are you withholding information? Are you being dishonest?

Telling a child they are adopted is best tackled at a very early age and in an informal manner. There are many different everyday life situations that can be used to start this process. Young children are far more accepting of information without question than older children and this gives a sound base to give more graduated in depth explanation as your child develops.

Remember how to eat that elephant?

Small, simple chunks, that's the way to feed information. Start with the simple fact that you did not make or give birth to your child.

Look out for pregnant women their presence will help you no end!

It could be someone in your family or on the television or in a magazine, seek them out, don't wait for them to appear. Explain to your child that the pregnant woman has a big tummy because she and her partner have made a baby and it is growing inside her. Tell your child you didn't make them and they didn't grow in your tummy or your partner's tummy, they grew in another mummy's tummy. Tell them the name of their birth mother, saying you grew in ....'s tummy. Tell them growing in one mummy's tummy then having a different mummy to look after them is called ADOPTION. Tell them they are ADOPTED. This way of explaining can be adapted to suit older children

You are no longer under starter's orders, you're off!

Following on from the initial telling of adoption your child will need explanation as to why this has happened and what it all means.

If your child has a Family History Book you can begin 'dipping' into this in the same way you would select a story book to read. Again this needs to be undertaken in small, simple chunks.

Explaining about parenting and what this entails is also a very good platform for informing your child of the reasons why they were separated from their birth family and adopted. This part of the process will assist in the building of your child's genetic identity and offering positive images of their birth family thus helping to build their own self esteem.

This is important in terms of your child's lifelong emotional security.

Explaining the concept of parenting needs some thought and creativity.

Using Fahlberg's 3 part parenting model in 'A Child's Journey through Placement—BAAF 1994' will prove to be invaluable.

You could also use What Does Adopted Mean: A Young Child's Guide to Adoption—Nicholls, 2005' which contains a child friendly version of Fahlberg's model.

Whatever method you use to explain the basics make it fun for and interesting to your child.

Explaining Why

Of course the telling process doesn't stop at explaining adoption and what it means, children need an explanation as to why it happened to them. This applies to older children placed for adoption who have some understanding of their past and current status but will need to know more of the why as they grow.

We are back to the elephant once again but this time the question is:

How do you eat a tough and indigestible elephant?

In explaining to your child the reason why you will probably have to talk about what could be termed 'adult matters'.

Examples of which are sexual abuse, incest, rape, domestic violence, drug and alcohol abuse and so on.

Not the usual topics of conversations one would have with young children and they are in many ways akin to trying to eat a tough and indigestible elephant!

So the answer to the question is:

You cut the elephant into small chunks then you cook the chunks until they are tender enough to eat.

Explaining adult matters to children needs for those matters to be 'cooked' until they are tender enough, presented in age appropriate terms, to give to your child.

If you need help in converting matters to age appropriate terms you could ask the agency's adoption support social worker for assistance. Use the FOG index which is a formula for calculating readability of text. There are likely to be some books on converting language to the level of children's understanding and ability, try the internet for help.

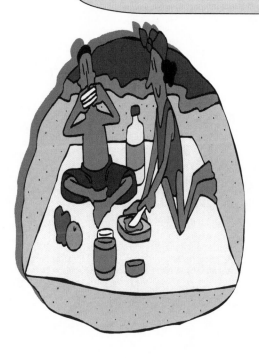

The way in which you serve information to your child, in other words chunks of tenderised elephant, will change according to your child's needs, level of maturity and ability to understand.

There will eventually come a day when your child can digest the raw truth, in other words a rare elephant steak, with little trouble because they have grown accustomed to the taste.

But Why?

But why did she take drugs?

But why didn't she want me?

But why did they do that to me?

But why couldn't they change?

But why was he so violent?

But why were they like that?

There are many, many more 'but whys' the above are just a few examples.

Giving reasons why your child's birth family acted in the way they did can become a minefield of judgemental values and blame if care is not taken.

In this early stage of the process of informing and explaining keeping the reasons why as simple as possible is the key. Whatever the circumstances that led to your child being separated from their birth family they can be explained by five easy to understand umbrella categories.

The Reasons Why

- ♦ Their birth parents may have problems or troubles that makes it really difficult for them to care for others and do all the tasks of parenting.

- ♦ They may never have been taught how to parent or look after or care for others.

- ♦ They may be too ill to be a parent or care for others.

- ♦ They may not be able to learn how to be a parent or care for others.

- ♦ They may have been shown the wrong way to parent or care for others.

The reason for your child's separation from birth family will fit into one or even a number of the above categories.

Avoid at all costs using the 'ill' category as a cover all or a euphemism for something else. It confuses children and it will confuse you when the child starts asking when the birth parent will get better.

If the reason is genuinely illness then an explanation as to the nature of that illness is needed and why a birth parent would not recover or get well enough in time to parent and care for the child.

SOME FINAL THOUGHTS ABOUT THE TELLING PROCESS

- ◆ Talking to your children about adult matters is no easy task even in usual circumstances.

- ◆ In adoption this task appears more complex because it could have far reaching implications for the positive promotion of your children's genetic identity, lifelong emotional security and your relationship with them.

- ◆ But the consequences of not telling has an even greater significance.

- ◆ You know your children better than anyone and you will know the right time for the 'when, what, where, how, who and why'.

And finally...

- ◆ Whatever your fears or concerns are about the telling process always bear in mind your children trust and love you as you do them. What better starting point could anyone wish for.

'Life can only be understood
backwards;
But it must be lived forwards.'

-Sören Kierkegaard
1813-1855

REFERENCES

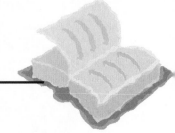

BAAF.1998, *Exchanging Visions : Papers on Best practice in Europe for Children Separated from their Birth Families*. London: BAAF.

Bowlby, J. 1988, *A Secure Base: Clinical Applications of Attachment Theory*. London: Routledge.

Brodzinskey, D, et al.1993, *Being Adopted: The Lifelong Search for Self*. New York: Anchor Books.

DoH. 1998, *Quality Protects: Transforming Children's Services*.

Fahlberg, V. 1987,*Helping Children when they must Move*. London: BAAF.

Fahlberg, V. 1994, *A Child's Journey Through Placement*. London: BAAF.

HMSO.1985, *Social Work Decisions in Child Care. Recent Research Findings & their Implications*.

Hoghughi, M. 1978,*Troubled and Troublesome: Coping with Severely Disturbed Children*. London: Burnet Books.

Nash, R.1973, *Classrooms Observed: Perception and Pupils Performance*. London: Routledge & Kegan Paul,

Nicholls, E.A.2005**(a)**, *What Does Adopted Mean? A Young Child's Guide to Adoption*. Lyme Regis: Russell House Publishing.

Nicholls, E.A. In pub. *My Memory Book for Babies and Toddlers*. 2005**(b)**, *My Memory Book for children age 4+*. In pub.*My Memory Book for children age 8+*. Lyme Regis: Russell House Publishing.

Ryan, P & Walker, R.1985, *Life Story Work,* 2003, revised edition. London: BAAF.

Schoenberg et al. 1970, *Loss and Grief*. Columbia University Press: USA.

Winnicott, C. 1986, Face to Face with Children. In Batty, D. (Ed.) *Working with Children*. London:BAAF.

IMPLEMENTING THE MODEL, DEVELOPMENT AND TRAINING

Implementing the model, as with any other change of policy and practice, begins with management approval. Before approval there has to be knowledge and informing the various tiers of management of the benefits of the New Life Work Model is the first stage. I found that a short PowerPoint presentation of approximately 15 minutes with an equally short question and answer session helped inform and generate interest. The presentation was then given to practitioners, corporate partners, and temporary carers.

Implementation can be a graduated process. Begin simply with the provision of memory books to all looked after children and the rest will follow.

For smaller independent organisations and agencies it might be helpful to network and pool resources in presentations and training programmes.

Training for temporary primary carers and those professionals who are likely to be more directly involved in the processes and components of the New Life Work Model is significant in the implementation of the model. However, implementation can begin prior to training programmes.

Providing practitioners and carers understand the processes of the model, training can follow on. It is essential to include a small module within the pre-approval training of carers to raise awareness and understanding of the model.

I have created two training courses, one for carers and one for professionals. I have also created the PowerPoint presentations for management approval, informing practitioners, carers and corporate partners, and for inclusion in pre-approval training. So there really isn't any need to 're-invent the wheel', although agencies may well want to adapt this particular 'wheel' to suit their individualism.

I am available for consultation on implementing the model and its inclusion in the pre-approval training of carers and adopters, or for any queries you may have.

If you would like information about the above you can contact me by e-mail on EdithNicholls@aol.com